1

A MAGICAL VIEW from planet EARTH

Have you ever gazed up at night and been amazed at the stars twinkling above your head?

Every night, as you brush your teeth and prepare for bed, something magical is happening outside your bedroom window. As the sky darkens, thousands of stars emerge and are laid out like a carpet of jewels. The stars are joined by beaming planets, swift shooting stars, glittering star clusters, and many other exciting cosmic personalities. An orchestra of light and color is waiting for you, if only you peek around the curtains.

I fell in love with stargazing when I was your age and discovered a fascinating new world. The more I learned, the more familiar I became with the stars I could see from my home in England. My favorite *constellations* (imaginary shapes in the stars) were Cassiopeia, which looks like a "W" in the sky, and the Great Bear. But now that I live on the other side of the world, in Australia, I can't see those familiar shapes at all. I've had to discover completely new constellations, like Sagittarius, which looks like a teapot, and the Southern Cross.

Fun Fact

Stargazing is an awe-inspiring hobby that is fun to learn. For me, it also led to an exciting career as an astrophysicist, a scientist who studies the stars, which has enabled me to travel the world and discover new things about our universe!

Whether it's for fun or study, getting started with stargazing is easy, especially when you have an expert guide. And I've got you covered there!

Fun Fact

The Earth is not a perfect sphere, like a basketball. Because it spins on its axis and has liquid insides, the Earth is fatter around the equator than around the poles. The fancy name for its shape is an *oblate spheroid*.

As a child, Dad and I would tiptoe into our backyard under the cover of darkness and look up to experience a breathtaking dome of twinkling lights. Now that I'm grown up, I still spend many evenings watching the stars—from the beach, my yard, and even mountaintops.

Why do we see different stars around the world?

For tens of thousands of years, people have created stories based on the stars. They are used to navigate land and sea, predict weather and seasons, locate food and water, and are cultural and spiritual anchors. As people began to travel the world, they shared these stories while they gathered around campfires at night.

It became clear to these travelers more than 2500 years ago that the stars visible from the Northern Hemisphere of Earth, above the *equator*, are completely different from those seen from the Southern Hemisphere, below the equator. Ancient scientists noticed that as you get closer to the equator you start to see more and more of the constellations from the other hemisphere of the sky. That's how people first realized that the Earth is round.

Day and night

The Earth *orbits* the Sun. At an average distance of 93 million miles, it is still close enough for us to feel the kiss of the Sun's heat and light, enabling plants to grow and animals—including us—to live.

At any one time, half the Earth's surface faces the Sun. There, it is daytime. The other half faces away from the Sun. This, of course, is called nighttime. Since the Earth is continually spinning on its *axis*, the boundary between night and day is always moving.

Fun Fact

The Sun is our very own star; a gigantic ball of gas that burns by a process called *nuclear fusion*. Deep in the Sun's core, tiny particles of hydrogen combine to make helium, giving off heat and light, which is beamed into space in all directions.

Have you ever noticed that the Sun rises in the east and sets in the west? That's because our planet is constantly spinning from west to east, making one full revolution each day. Since everything around us is also spinning, including the ground and the air, we don't feel the movement at all. To us, it seems like we are standing still, and the Sun is traveling across the sky.

How long is a day?

OK, this one is easy. It's 24 hours, right?

Well, it's not quite as simple as that. The time it takes for the Earth to spin once on its axis is 24 hours, as viewed from the Sun.

This is called a *solar day* ("solar" means something relating to the Sun). But that's not the only way to measure the length of a day.

If you traveled far away from the Earth and viewed it from the stars, it would take 23 hours, 56 minutes, and 4 seconds for any place on the Earth to perform one complete rotation. This period is called a *sidereal day*—"sidereal" (sigh-*dear*-ee-al) means relative to the stars.

Why is a sidereal day almost 4 minutes shorter than a solar day? It's because the Earth moves around the Sun a little bit each day, so it takes an extra 4 minutes for the Earth's surface to line up with the Sun once again. That's why your favorite star will rise, on average, 4 minutes earlier each day.

Fun Fact

There is no up or down in space. It is an illusion caused by gravity, which pulls us towards the center of the Earth wherever we are on the planet's surface. That's why you don't feel upside down when you're in Australia, South America, Antarctica, or southern Africa, even though it might seem so when you look at a traditional globe, which has north at the top and south on the bottom.

The length of a solar day varies slightly throughout the year. In mid-December we are slightly closer to the Sun and the solar day is up to 30 seconds longer. In March and September, the solar day is around 20 seconds shorter.

To keep it simple, we average everything out to 24 hours for our calendar. Weird or what?

Years and years

A year is the time it takes for the Earth to make one complete orbit around the Sun. But did you know that this orbit takes 365.25 days?

To make our calendar simpler, we pretend that there are exactly 365 days in a year and then we add an extra day—February 29—every 4th year to catch up, which we call a *leap year*. People born on February 29 miss out on a lot of birthdays!

The Earth takes a slightly non-circular path around the Sun, called an *ellipse* (el-*ips*). At the closest point to the Sun, which happens in January, we are "only" 91.4 million miles from our star. At the farthest point in our orbit, which happens in July, the Earth is 94.5 million miles away. That's over a 3-million-mile difference! Oddly enough, though, this is *not* what causes the seasons.

What's the reason for the season?

Our planet is a bit wonky. There, I said it. The axis of the Earth is off-kilter, tilted at an angle of 23.5 degrees from upright compared with our orbit around the Sun.

For 6 months of the year, the Northern Hemisphere points towards the Sun, while for the other 6 months, the Southern Hemisphere enjoys its full attention. When your hemisphere points towards the Sun, the sunlight is stronger, days are longer, and the weather is warmer. Grab your shorts and T-shirts, it's finally summer!

Winter is the opposite: when your part of the Earth points away from the Sun, the heat and light are weaker, the days are shorter, and temperatures cooler. Brrrrr! In-between summer and winter are spring and fall, when both hemispheres receive equal love and attention from our star.

The Earth is not alone in having a lopsided tilt as it glides around the Sun. Mars, Saturn, and Neptune have a similar wonky axis, meaning they experience seasons just like we do. You can see the seasons of these planets with your own eyes by watching the changing angle of Saturn's rings or observing Mars's polar ice caps advance and retreat over several years. Mercury and Jupiter have better-behaved orbits and therefore, have no such seasonal cycles.

Venus rotates at an angle of almost 177 degrees, meaning it is almost perfectly upside down compared with the other planets. We don't know how this came about, but it's probably due to a major crash between Venus and another rocky body billions of years ago, during the formation of the *solar system*, which is made up of the Sun and all the planets, moons, and asteroids. A similar event probably turned Uranus on its side—this planet's axis lies at an angle of around 98 degrees.

Fun Fact

Many parts of the world have 4 seasons: spring, summer, fall, and winter. But the tropics (regions of the Earth close to the equator) have 2 major seasons: wet and dry. That's because equatorial regions get plenty of sunshine year-round. This creates a lot of rainfall, followed by a long dry period. First Nations people in tropical regions of Australia describe 6 seasons, based on the changing weather, wind direction, and behavior of birds and animals.

Sun on the run

The planets aren't the only things on the move. Our solar system is zipping around the center of the *Milky Way*, which is our galaxy—a stupendous megacity made up of an estimated 200 billion stars. The Milky Way has spiral arms made of stars and gas curled around its center, like an octopus. They are a fabulous sight for stargazers.

Over the coming hundreds of thousands of years, future generations will slowly witness a mass reshuffle of the

Fun Fact

Traveling at an eye-watering speed of 137 miles per second, it takes the solar system around 230 million years to make one complete journey around our spiral home. This is known as 1 galactic year.

familiar stars in the night sky as they move around the Milky Way. All the constellations we know and love will eventually dissolve.

It just goes to show that nothing in this universe lasts forever.

Top 5 facts about the view from Earth

1 The stars visible from above the equator are different from those seen below the equator because the Earth is round.

2 The Earth is not a perfect sphere and the technical name for its shape is an oblate spheroid.

3 The Sun rises in the east and sets in the west because our planet is constantly spinning to make one full revolution each day.

4 The Earth has seasons because its axis is wonky, so different parts of our planet point towards the Sun throughout the year.

5 The solar system circles the Milky Way every 230 million years, known as 1 galactic year.

2

LET'S get STARGAZING

Constellations

People have studied the night sky for many thousands of years, trying to make sense of what they see. Our ancestors saw figures in the shapes made by the brightest stars and told stories to describe how they interacted with our world. These constellations are important because they connect us to our past. They are also very practical as markers in the sky that tell those living traditional lifestyles when to plant, gather, and harvest food, and help people navigate long distances.

Fun Fact

The stars that make up constellations are not really "groups" of stars, nor are they clustered together by gravity. They may look like they are close to one another in the sky from our vantage point on the Earth, but many of them are trillions of miles apart. Far out!

Each cultural group has its own names for constellations, ranging from the Black Tortoise of China to the Giraffe of southern Africa. Some nations see constellations not in the stars but in the dark spaces between them. Famous dark constellations include the Emu in the Sky, important to many First Nations people in Australia, and the Llama, Frog, and Snake of the ancient Incan culture in South America. There are so many star stories and traditions that you could spend a lifetime investigating them all.

The 88 so-called *modern constellations* are used by scientists around the world to describe regions of the sky. Many of these star shapes are based on ancient Mesopotamian and Greek stories. However, they are no more "correct" than any other culture-based shapes in the stars, or even celestial characters that you choose to invent yourself.

Now that we've learned the basics, let's get stargazing!

How to start stargazing

First, choose a safe and comfortable stargazing spot. It could be in your yard, on your balcony, or in a neighborhood park. Take an adult with you—they are good for company, can carry stuff, and you can teach them about astronomy too! Now turn off any outdoor lights and find the darkest spot you can. You can set up a chair or a beach chair to make the experience even more comfy. Don't forget to wear suitable clothing, like warm clothes in winter and long sleeves to protect against mosquitoes in summer.

Thousands of stars are visible to the naked eye, which means it's easy to get overwhelmed. So how do you learn what you're looking at? How do you identify exciting things like planets, galaxies, comets, and shooting stars? Well, the first thing you're going to need is a star map.

Star maps

A map of the stars is not the same as a regular map. It won't show you the positions of local towns or cities, coastlines or national boundaries. Instead, a star map lays out the stars and constellations in the night sky. If you look very carefully, you will also find hidden gems like planets, galaxies, comets, satellites, and sparkling clusters made up of thousands of stars—we will meet those in Chapter 9.

When I was finding my way around the night sky, there were no computers or

Fun Fact

Since the Earth is constantly moving and spinning through space, our view of the stars changes hour by hour and night by night. So don't be surprised if the stars appear "upside down" or "sideways" compared with a star map. And don't worry, the stars stay in the same place relative to one another—at least over a human lifetime, so with a bit of practice you can learn to recognize the brightest stars, whichever way up they appear.

smartphones, and websites and apps hadn't been invented yet! My childhood star maps were printed on paper and bound into a big, chunky book called a *star atlas*. That meant wrangling thick bundles of paper in the dark, with a flashlight, and not having much of an idea which stars were currently above the horizon.

Nowadays, electronic devices make things a lot simpler. There are many excellent astronomy websites and apps to make stargazing easier. Here are some of the best.

A stargazing website

Stellarium (stellarium-web.org) is an awesome website that is also downloadable as an app and offers an interactive view of the sky, at any time and from any location on the Earth. Type in the name of your closest town or city and get ready to explore the stars and planets that will be visible tonight. You can track spacecraft and prepare for astronomical events like *meteor showers*, where many shooting stars appear on a certain night, or *eclipses*, where the Sun disappears behind the Moon, or the Moon disappears into the Earth's shadow.

You can zoom in or out, visualizing the whole sky as a circular dome, like a planetarium, or spying individual objects in detail. Click and drag any point on the map to see what the night sky looks like in a particular direction. On the horizon you can see all the compass directions, which helps you orient yourself.

Stellarium is a wonderful tool for scouting the night sky. Touch the galaxy icon to show *deep sky objects* on the map, meaning fainter objects like galaxies, gas clouds, and star clusters. Click on any star, planet, or other object to find out interesting facts, including its brightness (called *magnitude*—see page 130 for more info), distance, size, and much more.

Fun Fact

For mapping purposes, we imagine the night sky as a giant ball of stars around the Earth. We call it the *celestial sphere.* "Celestial" means "of the sky" in the ancient Roman language of Latin.

Constellation outlines can be turned on or off, depending on whether you want an uninterrupted view of the stars and planets, or you want to learn which constellations slot in where. For nighttime observing, select "night mode:" the screen will go red, a color that preserves your night vision. You can use the search feature to find almost any object in the night sky.

Best of all, you can set any location in the world and explore what the stars look like from Brazil, Botswana, Berlin, or Bangkok! Have some fun playing around with the settings.

Your Turn

Open your night-sky app and hold the phone up to the sky in any direction. On the screen, you'll get a real-time interactive map of exactly what's in front of you. They have a search tool for finding your favorite objects, and the star maps are clickable so that you can learn more about any interesting things you find. Many night-sky apps have an augmented-reality feature to display the real stars in front of the smartphone camera overlaid with a star map. So, let's go. Download a night-sky app today and get exploring!

Stargazing apps

There are some great night-sky apps for a smartphone or tablet that give you access to maps of the night sky for wherever you live on planet Earth. An advantage of these apps is that they are portable, easy to use, and allow you to stand outside and point a phone right at a star, planet, or constellation to identify and find out more about it.

Many night-sky apps are available for smartphones or tablets. I use Sky Guide, SkyView, and Stellarium, but also worth a look are Star Walk, Night Sky, Star Chart, SkyWiki, and Sky Map. Try a few and see what's right for you.

Sounds like space

There are fun ways to explore the universe using senses other than sight.

Touch the Universe is an astronomy book that helps visually impaired people experience the wonders of the universe. It uses a combination of braille and large-print captions that face 14 pages of brilliant Hubble Space Telescope photos, and it is embossed with shapes that represent various astronomical objects, such as stars, gas clouds, and jets of gas streaming into space.

Look It Up

Another great place to explore is NASA's sonification website chandra.si.edu/sound. There, scientists have turned pictures taken by NASA's telescopes into mesmerizing sounds. Check it out!

Top 5 apps and websites to explore

1 stellarium-web.org

2 Sky Guide

3 Sky View

4 Star Walk

5 chandra.si.edu/sound

3

YOUR CONSTELLATION
compendium

From a really dark observing site with an unobstructed horizon all around, you might see up to 4,500 stars with the naked eye. Unless you live in the wilderness, though, your night sky is probably brightened by streetlights. We call this *light pollution*, and it's a big problem for stargazers—and for our planet. Since the sky in our towns and cities is so light-polluted, people there may only see a few hundred of the brightest stars.

But never fear. Even if you're just looking out of your bedroom window with the lights turned off, you can still enjoy the best and brightest constellations in the

Fun Fact

Shining light into places where it's not needed, such as into the sky, onto buildings, and in rural areas, is bad for the animals, birds, and insects that rely on the natural cycle of day and night to feed, navigate, breed, migrate, and sleep. The best lighting is energy efficient, and it's shielded so that the light only goes where it is needed.

night sky. Be patient, give your eyes time to adjust to the darkness. After about 10 minutes, you will be able to see many more stars.

Wherever you end up viewing the universe, this book will help you explore the magnificent stars and constellations of the northern and southern skies.

Your Turn

In urban areas, with an adult for company, scout for a dark-sky site at places like parks, beaches, or find an unlit spot in the shadow of a wall, tree or building—you can also visit **darksitefinder.com**. You might even persuade your adult to take you on a countryside stargazing adventure on a clear night, "Please …it's educational!"

Orion

The constellation of Orion (the Hunter) is visible from almost everywhere on the Earth. If you live in a tropical region, you will see this magnificent constellation every night. The further from the equator you live, the longer you'll have to wait to see this superstar of the skies!

Orion has a very striking pattern. Seen from the Northern Hemisphere, it takes the form of a mythical hunter, with a club and a shield. Orion's body is marked by 4 vivid stars, including Betelgeuse, which is deep orange in color. Across the middle lies Orion's belt: a diagonal sweep of 3 stars, and hanging from his belt is a fainter trio known as Orion's sword.

From the Southern Hemisphere, the hunter appears the other way up. This is true for any constellation that's visible from both hemispheres—even for the Moon, as we will see in Chapter 6.

This is because when you cross the equator, you look at the sky from the opposite perspective.

Orion is a handy signpost for many interesting astronomical objects. Follow Orion's belt in a straight line to find Sirius, in the constellation of Canis Majoris (the Big Dog)—the brightest star in the whole sky. Follow his belt in the other direction to find the deep orange star Aldebaran (al-*deb*-er-an), in the constellation of Taurus (the Bull).

Fun Fact

In many traditional stories told in south-eastern Australia, the character whom the Greeks called Orion is known as Baiame, a creation ancestor, and he carries a boomerang. The story goes that Baiame was chasing an emu when he tripped and fell, which is why he appears upside down.

Further from Orion, you'll find the Pleiades (*ply*-a-deez), a glorious cluster of very young blue stars. Many people can see 6 of these stars with the naked eye, although some can distinguish all 7. How many can you see? Don't forget to use Stellarium or a night sky app to explore these objects and more!

The Southern Cross

If you live in the Southern Hemisphere, the most recognisable constellation is the Southern Cross, known in Latin as Crux Australis. Although it's the smallest of the modern constellations, the Southern Cross is famous, featuring on the flags of many countries, including Australia, New Zealand, Samoa, Papua New Guinea, and Brazil. It is made up of 4 bright stars: Acrux, Mimosa, Gacrux, and Imai. One of these stars is slightly orangey in color. Can you see which one?

Wrapping around the Southern Cross is Centaurus, a half-human, half-horse figure. Those ancient Greeks had quite an imagination! Its 2 brightest stars, Alpha and Beta Centauri, are called the Pointers since they are often used as markers to find the Southern Cross.

If you live more than 35 degrees south of the equator—in New Zealand, southern Australia, Argentina, or Chile—the Southern Cross is always visible.

Your Turn

We can't always rely on technology to help us navigate. What if your battery runs out, or there's no signal... or your tether breaks during a spacewalk and you float off? Here's a way to find due south without a compass or smartphone. Find the point in the sky where a straight line along the long axis of the Southern Cross meets a straight line at right angles to the line joining the Pointers. This is the South Celestial Pole. Drop down to the horizon and, ta da! ... Due south.

A pair of polar bears

Lost in the wilderness or adrift at sea? Look for the Pole Star, or Polaris, which has been helping people navigate the Northern Hemisphere for thousands of years. Polaris lies exceedingly close to the North Celestial Pole, meaning that it is perfect for direction-finding. It is the brightest star in the constellation of Ursa Minor (the Little Bear), which spins around the North Celestial Pole like a carousel ride at an amusement park.

Accompanying this dizzy little bear cub is the majestic Ursa Major (the Great Bear). This well-loved character contains 7 brilliant stars in a shape known alternatively as the Plough, the Big Dipper, or the Saucepan! I'll let you decide which name you use. The 2 bright stars on the right-hand side of the Plough are called Merak and Dubhe, and they point directly up to Polaris.

On the other side of the North Celestial Pole is Cassiopeia (Cassie-oh-*pee*-ah), a wonky W-shaped group of stars that represented the Queen of Ethiopia in ancient Greek mythology. Also twisted around Polaris is the curvy constellation Draco (*Dray*-co; the Dragon), and the faint and boxy Cepheus (*See*-fee-us), the King of Ethiopia. Northern sky-watchers can explore these constellations every night, since they never set.

Fun Fact

Over thousands of years, the Earth's axis will wobble and point in different directions. The fancy name for this movement is *axial precession*, and it is caused by the gravitational pull of the Moon and the Sun on the Earth's belly. It takes around 26,000 years for one lap to be completed, during which time the North and South Celestial Poles slowly make a circle around the sky, before ending up back where they began.

Your Turn

Hold your hand out in front of you at arm's length. The width of your pinkie finger is around 1 degree. Your thumb is about 2 degrees across. Now hold your middle 3 fingers together: that's 5 degrees. A scrunched-up fist is about 10 degrees across, and an outstretched hand span is approximately 20 degrees. Test it yourself by measuring the width of the Plough/Big Dipper (20 degrees) or the long axis of the Southern Cross (6 degrees).

The brightest constellations of the north

Once you are familiar with the Great Bear, you can use it to find other amazing constellations that light up Northern Hemisphere skies.

Next to the Great Bear is the constellation of Auriga, the Charioteer—although I think it looks more like a face of a king, wearing a crown. You can see this magnificent stellar grouping from the tropics or the Northern Hemisphere.

Look 40 degrees below the Great Bear's body to find the striking figure of Leo (the Lion). If you can make out a lion, you are doing better than me! Personally, I think it looks like a backwards question mark, with the constellation's brightest star, Regulus, as the dot.

Between Auriga and Leo is Gemini (the Twins). 2 bright stars, Castor and Pollux, stand out, with many fainter stars forming the body, arms, and legs of these mythical siblings.

The tail of the Great Bear points to the radiant red star Arcturus in the constellation of Boötes (bo-*oh*-tease), which reminds me of a kite soaring high on a breezy day. Beside Boötes lies the slender northern crown constellation, Corona Borealis.

Your Turn

Look for the small but charismatic constellation Delphinus (the Dolphin). You can almost imagine it leaping happily above ocean waves. It's one of the few constellations that actually looks like the thing it is named after!

Not too far away is the Flying Swan constellation, Cygnus. The long, slender shape of this celestial waterbird is quite beautiful. Close by, you can't miss the vivid blue star Vega in the tiny constellation of Lyra (the Harp).

A scorpion in your tea

2 fabulous constellations for those living south of the equator to find on a winter evening are Scorpius (the Scorpion) and Sagittarius (the Archer). They are also visible in the Northern Hemisphere up to about 40 degrees latitude, although they remain quite close to the horizon and can only be seen for a few weeks in the height of summer.

Scorpius soars magnificently high in Southern Hemisphere skies between June and July. Its main features are its brightest star, the deep-red Antares, and the elegant curve of the scorpion's stinging tail. After you first see it, it becomes unmistakable.

Perilously close to the scorpion's stinger is Sagittarius. If you include all the faint stars in the constellation, you end up with a half-man, half-horse with an archery hobby. But for most of us it is simply the Teapot, named after the most vivid stars which trace out the shape of this everyday household item.

Start your rocket engines. It's stargazing time!

These are just a few of the brilliant stars and constellations you can explore. Start your rocket engines, because you're now ready to begin your stargazing adventures for real. Check the weather forecast—clouds are not your friend—and don't forget to use the Stellarium website and the apps I've mentioned to look deeper into the night sky above you!

Fun Fact ☺

Something incredibly dark and powerful lives inside Sagittarius: a supermassive black hole that weighs more than 4 million times as much as the Sun! It's called Sagittarius A*. A* stands for "A-Star" and it marks the center of the Milky Way galaxy. But you can't see it because it's black, and hidden deep inside a dark cloud of space dust. You'll have to use your imagination!

Top 5 tips for getting started on your stargazing mission

1 Get your bearings by identifying 2 or 3 key constellations.

2 Visit Stellarium to help with preparations and important information.

3 Download your chosen apps.

4 Check the weather—cloudy nights are NOT ideal.

5 Find a location with the least amount of light pollution and allow your eyes to adjust to the darkness.

STARGAZING kit

I'll never forget the first time I saw Saturn through a telescope.
I was 13 years old and my mom had taken me to a local stargazing
night. It was held in a very dark place, deep in the English countryside
and they had a gigantic telescope that was bigger than me! To my
naked eye, Saturn looked like a gleaming yellow point of light. But
through this tremendous telescope, it transformed into a golden
cosmic bauble, encircled by a thousand delicate rings. The sight
was truly breathtaking.

You don't need a fancy kit to learn the constellations, marvel
at the Moon, spot shooting stars, and gaze at the brightest planets.
But a telescope will bring thousands of objects within your sight,
and reveal details of planets and moons that will astound you.

Where to start

I am often asked by beginner stargazers: "What telescope should I buy?"

My answer? Don't rush out and buy a telescope. Start with a pair of binoculars.

Binoculars are the ideal beginner's tool for exploring the cosmos. They are easy to use, portable, and not too expensive. They have a large field of view, which means that you can see a lot of the sky at one time. And they are great if you don't have a lot of space at home for a bulky telescope.

Binoculars

A pair of binoculars is just 2 small telescopes stuck together side by side. They work by bending light in a way that tricks both your eyes and brain into thinking that an object is larger than it is.

Binoculars have a piece of curved glass at one end called a *lens*, which you point towards the sky. As the light from stars or planets passes through this lens, the curved glass bends it, bringing the image together inside the binocular tube. At the other end, the bit you look through, is a smaller lens called the *eyepiece*, which magnifies the light to make the object look bigger.

Inside the tube are a few wedges of glass called *prisms*. These correct the image after the lens has flipped it upside down—things certainly get messy inside binoculars! Altogether, this clever design gives you an image that is bigger, brighter, and (phew!) the right way up.

Which binoculars are best for stargazing?

To make your purchase worthwhile, I recommend binoculars with lenses at least 50 millimeters in diameter. This will make your astronomical treasure hunting all the more rewarding, since the objects you're looking at will appear bigger and brighter than they do viewed with the naked eye. If you can't get a pair of astronomical binoculars, the compact ones used for birdwatching are okay, although their smaller lenses don't collect as much light. They are best suited to brighter targets like the Moon and planets.

My first pair of binoculars was a well-loved, secondhand set that must have been at least 30 years old. I explored the night sky with them for many happy years. They had 10 times magnification and the lenses were 50 millimeters across—also referred to as 10 × 50s (ten by fifties), and they were superb for scanning lunar craters and spotting the 4 largest moons of Jupiter. I often wonder where those binoculars are today.

Even bigger binoculars are available; for example, 20 × 80s, which give 20 times magnification and have 80-millimeter-diameter lenses. These are excellent for stargazing, although they are heavier and harder to hold. In my opinion, 10 × 50s are a great choice for beginners.

If you can't hold your binoculars still, the stars will jump all over the place, so consider attaching them to a tripod. That will also leave your hands free for checking a night-sky app or taking pictures. With a little practice, you can take photographs by pointing your camera lens through the binocular eyepiece. Something to impress your friends!

Telescopes

A telescope will supercharge your view of the night sky. But there are many different types and the choice can get a bit overwhelming. Here's what you need to know.

Telescopes collect light using a lens or mirror pointed up at the sky. Telescopes with a mirror are called reflecting telescopes, or *reflectors*, and those with a lens are called refracting telescopes, or *refractors*. Whichever style you choose, keep in mind that the bigger the mirror or lens, the brighter the resulting image will be.

> **Fun Fact**
>
> Did you know that most telescopes flip the image of the night sky upside down? But don't worry, there is no "up" or "down" in space, so we just roll with it!

At the other end of the telescope, the light collected is magnified through an eyepiece to produce a zoomed-in picture. You can use different eyepieces depending on what you want to see. A wide-field eyepiece is ideal for viewing the Moon or a large cluster of stars, whereas a stronger eyepiece will zoom in to a small area of sky— perfect for studying things like galaxies or distant planets.

Mounted on the side of the telescope tube is a cute little *finderscope*, which helps you point the telescope at your chosen target.

Don't knock it

The image created by a telescope is magnified, so even a small movement, like accidentally touching the telescope tube, will make the image dance around the eyepiece. Nobody likes a wobbly star. To limit this problem, plant your telescope on the steady but moveable platform called a *mount*.

One of the most impressive telescope set-ups is a computerized mount, also known as a "go-to" system. This allows you to type in the name or celestial coordinates of any astronomical object. The computer attached to the mount will then drive the motors to point the telescope to exactly the right point in the sky.

Some people think this is cheating, but I must say it's a pretty neat invention. What stargazer wouldn't want to follow their target effortlessly through the sky as the Earth rotates and the stars move overhead?

What kind of telescope?

The best telescope is one you will use regularly.

If you have plenty of storage space, I'd recommend a reflecting telescope with a mirror at least 150 millimeters across. A Dobsonian mounted telescope—one that nods up-down and spins around—is a great place to start because it's easy to use. However, the bigger versions can be bulky and heavy, and they take a bit of time to set up, so be careful not to buy something that will sit in the garage gathering dust.

A more portable option is a tabletop reflecting telescope which, as the name suggests, can stand on top of a table, on a balcony or in the backyard. I would still recommend one with a mirror at least 150 millimeters across, since the results you get from smaller versions can be quite disappointing.

Another option is a refracting telescope. On the plus side, they are fairly light and portable, but the downside is that the lenses can distort the colors of stars and planets if they are not high quality.

If you stargaze while seated—for example, if you use a wheelchair—then a Dobsonian tabletop telescope or a refractor mounted on a surface at a suitable height may prove the most comfortable.

Get advice from an experienced observer and try before you buy. Visit your local astronomical society or attend a public astronomy night, where amateur astronomers share their telescopes with others in their community. Some public libraries have telescopes for hire.

And if you don't have a shiny new telescope right now, don't worry! I never had a telescope as a kid—they were just too expensive. A pair of binoculars will still bring you many happy years of astronomical adventuring.

Astrophotography

Astrophotography means taking photographs of the stars. It's very rewarding because it gives you a permanent record of the brilliant things you've seen on your stargazing adventures.

Instead of taking a quick pic of the stars, you leave the camera shutter open for longer, increasing the amount of light received from very faint stars to create a much brighter picture. We call this *long-exposure photography* because the camera is exposed to the starlight for a long time.

The best astrophotographs are generally taken with digital single-lens reflex (DSLR) cameras. These are the big, bulky cameras used by professional photographers. But smartphone camera technology is catching up quickly. You can now take some great pics with them too, if you know what you're doing. Let's roll up our sleeves and try it for ourselves.

Snapping stars with a smartphone

I recommend taking pictures of the stars with a smartphone to begin with because it's fun and simple to learn. I love getting outside on a clear night and capturing constellations like Orion and the Southern Cross, a faint comet, or the aurora australis (southern lights). And you can do it too.

It's not quite as simple as pointing your phone at the sky and taking a snap. You may find yourself looking at a black screen. But don't stress. There are many clever nighttime camera settings and apps that allow you to take long exposure photographs. With a bit of practice, I guarantee you will get great results.

When you take your photographs, the longer the exposure, the greater the chance that something exciting like an airplane, a satellite, or even a shooting star will sneak into the shot. An airplane will have red and green navigation lights on its wings,

> **Fun Fact**
>
> You can insert other subjects into the foreground of your astrophotographs to make them look even more spectacular. Trees, buildings, even yourself—whatever you like. Just don't forget to stand still!

which should show up as colored stripes; helicopters and drones should have these navigation lights too. A shooting star will look like a short, bright trail, occasionally with a little "explosion" at one end. A satellite is a bit more boring—it looks like someone has taken a white pen and drawn a straight line across the photograph.

Capturing star trails

Star trails are semicircular arcs of light that show up in very-long-exposure photographs of the night sky. They are caused by the stars appearing to move around the celestial pole as the Earth rotates on its axis. A 5-minute exposure time will yield small hints of the stars' movements. A 30-minute exposure will leave substantial trails. A very long exposure of 3 to 6 hours will give you a dramatic swirl of silver stellar arcs.

Notice how the star trails form a circle, where the stars at the center barely move while those around the edge have quite long arcing trails. Smack dab in the middle of your circle will be the North or South Celestial Pole, with virtually no trail at all. That's another good way to find the celestial pole, if you have enough patience!

Your Turn

Open the camera app on your phone and select the "nighttime," "astrophotography" or, if you have it, "expert" mode. If not, download an astrophotography app like NightCap Camera for iPhones or ProShot for Android phones, and choose "long exposure" or "star" mode. The mode names will vary (with ProShot, for example, use "light painting" mode), so check out the instructions for your app. Finish the setup for a long-exposure photograph by turning off the flash and focusing at infinity (∞).

Mount your phone on a tripod and point the camera towards the sky—preferably at something interesting! If you don't have a tripod, lean your phone against a sturdy object so that it stays still. Then, when you're ready, click the camera button and start taking your picture.

On many smartphones, you will be able to see the image compiling in real time on the screen, with the stars getting brighter and brighter the longer you leave the exposure running. Judge for yourself when the stars look bright enough. I recommend waiting around 20–30 seconds and then press the shutter button again to complete the snap.

If your image is blurry, use a self-timer mode or voice activation—for example, "Hey Siri/Google, take a picture"—to avoid jolting the camera when you touch the screen. If your image is too dark, open the shutter for longer. Don't be afraid to experiment with different settings until you get your perfect shot.

That's it. Your first cosmic photograph will be saved on your phone. How does it look?

Don't forget that for your longer astrophotography sessions you can plug your phone into a portable battery charger to avoid it conking out in the middle of capturing an amazing pic.

Using a professional camera

With a DSLR camera, you can get some amazing photographs of the night sky. If you're interested, there are many books, magazines, and websites about astrophotography using these professional cameras. With so much to explore, it would take a lifetime to learn it all. But making a start today means that your journey of learning is underway.

Top 5 tips for getting the best out of your stargazing kit

1 Don't feel like you need the newest and shiniest equipment. Secondhand or borrowed equipment will be fine.

2 Join your local Astronomical Society to benefit from meeting like-minded friends and to share equipment and knowledge.

3 Practice makes perfect when it comes to photographing the night sky.

4 Don't forget to charge your phone battery!

5 Books, magazines, and websites are a great source of information for getting started on your journey to learn more about the universe.

5

MEET the PLANETS

Since the solar system formed, the planets have been among the brightest objects in the night sky, despite them shining only by the reflected light of the Sun. Even today, they make the most glorious targets for all stargazers, from beginners to professionals. In 1992, my dad read an article in a newspaper that said Mars would be visible that night with the naked eye. Excited at the prospect of spotting the Red Planet, we waited until it was dark and, using a flashlight to illuminate our tiny star map, we oriented ourselves to the unfamiliar constellations. Finally, we saw it—a tiny orange globe that was more brilliant than the surrounding stars. I was gobsmacked that you could see a faraway planet without a telescope. The experience forever changed my view of the night sky.

Our solar system is rich with stargazing goodness. Even if the Earth's own star, the Sun, is a bit of a pest that overwhelms our view of the universe for around 12 hours each day. Our star is also pretty good at shining a light (get it!?) on the darker objects that lurk out in space. The planets, asteroids, comets, and moons of our solar system (yes, other planets have moons too) don't shine like the stars. They reflect light from the Sun, and without it, they would be completely invisible to us.

Around 4.6 billion years ago, our solar system formed from the *solar nebula*, a gigantic cloud of gases and tiny dust particles that was floating in space. Gravitational forces pulled the solar nebula together, and as it shrank, the cloud began spinning and formed a

flat disk, like a pancake. When clumps of the disk contracted, with gravity the culprit again, the Sun, planets, and moons were made. To this day, the flat disk remains, and all the planets orbit the Sun in the same direction. The great circle around our sky where the Sun, Moon, and planets appear is called the *ecliptic*.

Let's meet the planets of our solar system and learn how to observe them.

Mercury

Mercury is a small, rocky planet, only slightly bigger than our Moon. It is our star's closest friend, never leaving the Sun's side as it whizzes around in an 88-day orbit. The farthest Mercury ever gets from the Sun is 28 degrees, that's around 1 handspan and a fist. That's why the planet is only visible close to sunrise or sunset. We call this its *greatest elongation*. At greatest eastern elongation, Mercury is visible after sunset, and at greatest western elongation, it's visible before sunrise. I usually focus on the eastern elongation because I don't like getting up early. Who does!?

Look It Up

Jump on an astronomy website like **earthsky.org** to find out when Mercury will next be visible where you live.

To the naked eye, Mercury appears as a silvery dot of light peeking out of the twilight. Its brightness depends on how close the planet is to us, and how much of its disk is illuminated. You won't see much detail on Mercury with binoculars, and it doesn't have moons of its own, but a small telescope can reveal its changing phases as it swings around the Sun.

The position of Mercury changes all the time, so stay alert to catch its marvelous glimmer in our morning or evening skies.

Venus

Venus is the second planet from the Sun and it has no moons.

From the safety of planet Earth, Venus has to be one of the most spectacular sights in our night sky. It appears as a dazzlingly bright star-like object—some people mistake it for a UFO, making it a perfect target for any stargazer. The greatest elongation of Venus from the Sun is 47 degrees, so it's visible more often than Mercury.

As Venus orbits the Sun, which it does once every 225 days, different parts of the planet are illuminated by our star. The phases of Venus change from a big, slender crescent when the planet approaches the Earth, to a squat, curved shape when Venus reaches the farthest point of its orbit. Venus's phases can be seen through a good pair of binoculars, although a telescope will do a far better job.

Fun Fact

Venus is a similar size to Earth and is often described as "Earth's twin." That's a pretty far-fetched claim, though, because Venus is extremely hostile. Any spacecraft daring to land there would be simultaneously crushed by the pressure, melted by the intense heat, and dissolved in atmospheric acid. Gulp.

Fun Fact

We call Mercury and Venus the *inferior planets*. That doesn't mean they aren't as good as the other planets, just that they orbit closer to the Sun than the Earth does. The *superior planets* are those that lie farther from the Sun than we are. They take a lot longer to orbit the Sun, and their apparent size and brightness vary a lot as they do so.

Mars

Mars is often called the Red Planet. This is because its iron-rich soil and frequent dust storms make this distant world take on an orangey-red color.

Mars is a superior planet, so its distance from the Earth varies wildly. It *oscillates* between very big and bright when at *opposition*, which is the planetary equivalent of a full Moon, and quite small and distant as it shrinks behind the Sun at *conjunction*, which is similar to the new Moon. The distance to Mars can be as little as 35 million miles and as much as a whopping 250 million miles. The planet takes around 26 months to go from closest to furthest approach.

The polar ice caps of Mars can be spotted through most small telescopes, at least when the planet is close to opposition. They are made of frozen carbon dioxide and water ice and look like white disks at Mars's poles. With a medium-sized amateur telescope such as a 300-millimeter reflector, Mars's tiny asteroid moons, Phobos and Deimos, are faintly visible as 2 small flecks of light accompanying the planet.

Fun Fact

Viewed through a backyard telescope, Mars reveals many secrets. Light and dark patches can be seen on the planet's surface, showing regions where fine dust lies and darker rocks are exposed. Its surface features are occasionally hidden by massive dust storms that rage across the planet.

Jupiter

To our eyes, Jupiter appears yellowish-white. The solar system's largest planet is around 5 times farther away than the Sun is from us, but it makes up for it by sheer size—more than 300 Earths would fit inside. And because Jupiter's clouds reflect sunlight very well, the planet easily outshines the brightest stars in the night sky.

With binoculars, the planet's 4 brightest moons—Io, Europa, Callisto, and Ganymede—slip into view. They are the most easily visible of the planet's estimated 92 moons.

Jupiter looks even more magnificent through a small telescope, which reveals the planet's colorful cloud bands, and the Great Red Spot, a circulating weather system with wind speeds of more than 250 miles per hour.

The planet has many secrets. One is a faint set of rings made up of millions of dust particles, which was discovered by the space probe *Voyager 1* in 1979. Despite being more than 124,000 miles across (15 times the size of our planet), Jupiter's rings are completely invisible from Earth. Who knows what other secrets are yet to be found?

Saturn

As with any faraway planet, the best time to view our stunning ringed friend is around the time of opposition, which happens every 12½ months. Saturn looks like a bright yellow star to the naked eye and is easily viewed, even in light-polluted cities.

Unlike the faint, delicate, and invisible rings surrounding Jupiter, Saturn boasts a vast and complex system of ice and dust particles, which are so bright that you can spot them from your garden with a decent pair of binoculars.

Fun Fact

Did you know that all the planets beyond Mars in our solar system are mostly made of gas? That means they have no solid surface and landing on them would be impossible. Astrobiologists are scientists who study life in the universe and think it is very unlikely that these planets could support life.

Saturn has around 82 confirmed moons, the brightest of which is Titan. Bigger than the planet Mercury, Titan is visible through large binoculars (60 millimeters or larger) or a small telescope. Many of the moons are too faint to see from Earth but you can see more of the bright moons of Saturn, including Rhea, Tethys, Dione, Iapetus, Enceladus, and Mimas, through a 150-millimeter telescope.

Uranus

Uranus lives in the outer region of the solar system, far from the warmth of the Sun. Like all the planets beyond Mars, it is mostly made up of a mixture of cold chemical gases held together by gravity. Being such a distant mirror to the Sun, Uranus struggles to send enough light back to the inner solar system to be clearly seen from the Earth.

Uranus is a tricky target for amateur astronomers as it appears only very faintly to the naked eye once a year, coinciding with the planet's opposition. Even through binoculars or a telescope, it's still a difficult object to study due to a lack of features. It's really just a big blue blob! Any detection is a triumph—if you manage to see the very small, blue disk of Uranus, then you're doing very well indeed. With a large, at least 8-inch, telescope, you may be able to distinguish its 2 brightest moons: Titania and Oberon.

Neptune

The most distant world in our solar system is Neptune, shivering alone on average some 2.8 billion miles from the Sun. At this vast distance, each orbit takes Neptune 164.8 years. The planet is never visible to the naked eye.

Interestingly, Neptune was discovered in 1846, when astronomers realized that the orbits of the other planets were being diverted by the gravitational pull of a mysterious, unseen body. They did some calculations and predicted where the secret planet should lie. Lo and behold, there it was! Neptune was soon spotted by at least 3 independent observers.

Neptune is pretty featureless when seen from the Earth, appearing as a plain blue disk. Its faint rings and moons are not visible to most backyard telescopes.

Top 5 things to know about our planets

1 The position of Mercury changes all the time, so stay alert to catch its marvelous glimmer in morning or evening skies.

2 Venus is visible to the naked eye and is dazzlingly bright—some people mistake it for a UFO—making it a perfect target for any stargazer.

3 Mars has 2 tiny moons that are probably asteroids captured long ago by the planet's gravity.

4 Saturn boasts a vast system of ice and dust rings, which are so bright that you can spot them with a decent pair of binoculars.

5 With a telescope, Uranus just looks like a faint blue blob!

6

THE MOON: Earth's cosmic COMPANION

The beauty and grace of Earth's natural satellite has charmed our ancestors for tens of thousands of years. To some ancient cultures, the Moon was a god or goddess whose periodical activities brought us life. Whatever the cultural significance of the Earth's cosmic companion, it is always a tremendous sight for intrepid young stargazers—and that's you!

Every month, the Moon's orbit takes it on an elliptical path around the Earth. It takes 27.3 days to make one full journey—a sidereal month. And by no coincidence, the Moon also takes 27.3 days to do one full rotation on its axis. That's because gravity causes these 2 great lumps of rock to attract one another and holds their bulging bellies together. Scientists call this *tidal locking*, or *synchronous rotation*. Because of this, the same side of the Moon always faces the Earth—although the Moon's elliptical orbit means that we sometimes get to peek a little bit around the corner.

> ## Fun Fact
>
> The Moon doesn't quite "orbit" the Earth. They both orbit the Earth–Moon center of gravity, or the point where the Earth and Moon would balance, as if on a seesaw. This point lies on average 2902 miles from the center of the Earth— that's three-quarters of the way from the Earth's center to the surface!

It's just a phase

Because the angle between the Moon, Earth, and Sun is constantly changing, we see different portions of the Moon's illuminated side every day. It takes 29 days, 12 hours, 44 minutes, and 2.9 seconds, or a *synodic* month, to go from one full Moon to the next.

You may have noticed that this is different from the 27.3 day sidereal month. That's because the Earth is traveling around the Sun, so the Moon needs to voyage a little bit farther each month to get back to the same place in its cycle.

The full Moon happens when the Sun, Earth, and Moon are lined up in a row. On one side of you, the Sun sinks below the horizon. On the opposite side, the full Moon rises up. When the Moon is close to the horizon, it appears next to familiar objects in the landscape like trees and buildings. It's an awesome sight, because your brain thinks that the Moon is closer, and therefore bigger, than it actually is.

Right after the full Moon, the Sun, Earth, and Moon are no longer perfectly lined up. That's when the Sun illuminates our rocky companion slightly from one side. We call this a gibbous (*gibb*-us) Moon, which looks egg shaped. A few days later, we see a half-Moon (a semicircle), which we call the last quarter of the Moon's cycle. A few days later still, it becomes an ever-thinning crescent shape, before finally retreating into darkness. This is the new Moon, where no sunlit part of the Moon is visible from the Earth.

Your Turn

You can prove the moon is not actually larger than usual when viewed on the horizon. Hold out your hand at arm's length, closing one eye, and cover the Moon completely with your pinkie nail. Then do the same when the Moon is high up in the sky. You'll see that it looks the same size.

Fun Fact ☺

You may hear that the Moon is made of cheese (and I *love* cheese), but unfortunately, it's made of a light gray powdery rock dust called *regolith*. Although this doesn't taste great in a sandwich, it does reflect a lot of the sunlight falling onto it back up into space. That's why the Moon looks so bright and brilliant in our night sky.

After the new Moon, its phases advance back through the same stages: crescent, first quarter (which is a semicircle-shaped half-Moon), an egg-shaped gibbous Moon, and then the completely illuminated full Moon.

Fun Fact

The most heavily cratered region of the Moon is its far side—the Moon's backside—which permanently points away from the Earth. We had no idea what the far side of the Moon looked like until 1959, when the Soviet Union sent an uncrewed spacecraft called *Luna 3* around the back to take our very first pictures of this hidden region.

Look It Up

You can see detailed drawings of the Moon's phases on an excellent NASA website **moon.nasa.gov**.

Look It Up

Explore the Moon's mountains, craters, and plains in all their glory using websites such as Google Moon (google.com/moon) and NASA's fantastic Lunar Reconnaissance Orbiter (lunar.gsfc.nasa.gov).

Fun Fact

The Moon is the only place other than the Earth where human beings have set foot. The first astronauts from the United States traveled around 234,000 miles each way to walk—or bunny hop—on the Moon in 1969 and 1972. You can still see the equipment they left on the lunar surface, and even their footprints, in images captured by NASA's Lunar Reconnaissance Orbiter.

Your Turn

You might find it interesting to track the phases of the Moon throughout the month by setting up a moon diary. It takes a bit of patience but is well worth the effort to understand the ever-changing face of our friendly local space rock.

Draw the Moon on each clear day or night for a month, sketching its features and phases. If you're not sure where the Moon is, use Stellarium or a night-sky app to locate it. It's often visible during the day, especially around first and last quarter, otherwise known as half-Moon phases. Remember that it might be below the horizon right now, but that's OK: you can check out what time it rises and sets online (timeanddate.com/moon). Make sure you enter your location on the Earth when using the website, since the Moon rises and sets at different times in different places around the world.

If the Moon isn't visible right now because it's on the other side of the planet (understandable) or hidden by cloud (unlucky), don't worry. You can still study our pockmarked friend using some handy technological tools.

Taking a closer look

Our Moon is a stunning sight when seen with the naked eye, but it looks even better close up. If you don't have a pair of binoculars or a telescope, then jump online to explore Moon maps, or better still, go along to your local astronomy viewing night, because you don't want to miss this!

Observing the Moon magnified is like exploring a new world. You'll discover magnificent mountains, rocky plains, giant meteorite craters, serene seas … wait a minute. Seas? ON THE MOON? Well, OK, they're not watery seas, with friendly lunar dolphins splashing around in spacesuits. But they are called *Maria* (*marr*-ee-uh, the Latin word for "seas") because the Romans thought they might be seas, and the name stuck. We now know that the Maria are plains of molten lava that cooled and dried up billions of years ago, leaving behind large, flat areas of dark volcanic rock.

Early stargazers saw something else in the shapes on the surface of the Moon. Instead of a series of aquatic features, they imagined characters associated with cultural stories or the worship of Moon gods. In Asian and Native American folklore, the dark features are known as a mystical Moon rabbit, although I think it looks more like a crab. What creatures do you see on the Moon's volcanic plains?

One of the most spectacular sights on the Moon is its craters. Formed more than 4 billion years ago, when rocks from outer space regularly bombarded our natural satellite, the Moon's craters are rugged and beautiful. They range in size from smaller than a pea to more than 1,500 miles across. Many of the larger craters have a ring of mountains around their edge, and most have a flat base with a small mountain at its center, created at the time of the impact. In some cases, we also see bright rays of lighter-colored dust radiating out from the crater.

Fun Fact

The Moon is seen from opposite perspectives in the Northern and Southern Hemispheres of the Earth, although neither is "upside down" or the "right way up." If you are comparing maps with your own observations of the Moon, make sure that you search for information relevant to your hemisphere.

Photographing the Moon

Taking a good picture of the Moon at night is difficult because it is very bright against a dark background sky. Luckily, though, you can adjust the settings on your smartphone's camera app to get the best possible shot.

With professional equipment and a DSLR camera, you'll get much better results. Remember to keep the exposure time short, zoom in, and keep the tripod steady. Good luck!

Your Turn

For the best chance of taking a good picture of the Moon, set the camera up on a tripod to avoid any shakes. Turn the flash off and double-tap the screen to focus on the Moon. Zoom in a little to make the Moon appear bigger. If you have an exposure (EXP) setting on your camera app, turn it down until you're happy with how bright the Moon appears on-screen—it should look a bit silvery gray rather than brilliant white. Now you're ready to take your snap.

When to look

From the Earth, the surface features of the full Moon look washed out. Why? Because when the Moon is full, the Sun is almost overhead at the Moon, so the mountains and craters don't cast any shadows. A partial phase of the Moon makes it far more interesting, with lumps and bumps visible in the shadows trailing across its surface.

The terminator

The line between the light and dark zones of the Moon is called the *terminator*, which sounds exciting, and it is! It's packed with awesome craters, mountains, and valleys, and it looks truly spectacular through a pair of binoculars or a telescope.

Lunar eclipses

Every few months, somewhere on the Earth is treated to a lunar eclipse. This happens when the Earth is lined up directly between the Sun and the Moon. For a short time, around an hour or so, the full Moon darkens as it passes through the Earth's shadow.

This awesome astronomical event is sometimes called a *blood Moon*, because the Moon goes a deep red color. As the Sun's light filters through the Earth's atmosphere, the blue light is scattered across the sky while the red light continues, casting a tangerine hue across our celestial neighbor.

Fun Fact

The full Moon is more than 30,000 times brighter than Sirius, the brightest star in the sky. That's pretty amazing, since the Moon doesn't produce any light of its own. It could be even brighter, but the lunar soil is dark—reflecting less than one quarter of the sunlight that falls on its surface.

Look It Up

Jump online to timeanddate.com/eclipse/list-lunar.html and find out when the next lunar eclipse is due where you live.

Your Turn

Try sketching all the craters you can see along the terminator and compare your drawings with a detailed map of the Moon, which you can find online.

A lunar eclipse happens around every 2½ years in any given part of the world. It's a great time to try out your astrophotography skills, since the Moon is a lot fainter than usual and the colors are incredible.

Fun Fact

You might be wondering why a lunar eclipse doesn't happen more often. Surely the Sun, Earth, and Moon line up every month? Not quite. The Moon's orbit around the Earth is a little bit tilted compared with the Earth's orbit around the Sun, so they don't line up perfectly each month.

cheese this way

Top 5 things to know about the Moon

1 Every month, the Moon's orbit takes it on an egg-shaped path around the Earth which takes 27.3 days—also known as a sidereal month.

2 The full Moon is more than 30,000 times brighter than the brightest star and happens each month when the Sun, Earth, and Moon are lined up in a row.

3 To take a picture of the moon, put your phone on a tripod, turn the flash off, and focus on the Moon. Zoom in and turn down the exposure setting so the surface features are visible. Avoid shakes by using the timer or voice control to take the picture.

4 Peer at the Moon through binoculars or a telescope for a terrific view of the craters, mountains, and its other surface features.

5 A lunar eclipse happens around every 2½ years in any given part of the world, and you can see it with the naked eye as the full moon gradually darkens and turns red.

7

SPACE rocks!

Imagine the year is 1680. Electricity has not yet been discovered and there are no artificial lights. After dark, the sky is a deep inky canvas decorated with thousands of silver stars. One evening, you gaze up to see a strange new object, shining bright and wearing a glowing crown. Behind it trails a long white tail, flowing like a mane of hair. Each night it inches slowly across the sky, getting brighter as its locks unravel further.

Who is this interstellar interloper? A demon? A messenger from the gods?

Comets

Ancient people were often scared of comets, and I can understand why. When an unexpected, and kind of weird-looking, cosmic visitor turned up in the night sky, it seemed supernatural. But, thankfully, because of science, we have much better answers.

It turns out that comets are just big, dirty snowballs tumbling through space. They are made of rock and a mix of frozen chemicals called *ices*, which are materials left over from the formation of the solar system. On average, a comet is between a few several hundred feet to tens of miles across. Most have very long, elliptical orbits and spend much of their time far from the Sun, only rarely coming to visit the inner part of the solar system where we live.

When they venture into our neighborhood, the heat from the Sun melts the ices and turns them into gases. This forms the comet's atmosphere (called a *coma*) and tail. Both reflect the Sun's light, making them visible from the Earth. Once a comet retreats from the Sun, the gases freeze once again and the coma and tail disappear—the comet returns to being a dark, frozen rock, invisible to us. Seems sad, doesn't it?

Comets can be unpredictable stargazing targets. Some brighten dramatically when they approach the Sun, while others fizzle disappointingly. You never know what you're going to get. But this just adds to the thrill.

Fun Fact

We know what comets are made of because we've sent spacecraft to study them close up. During NASA's Deep Impact mission, a small device was slammed into the rocky core of a comet and the impact crater measured to see what types of rocks and chemicals were inside. NASA found the material was very fine, like talcum powder, and the chemicals suggested the comet had been formed outside the orbits of Uranus and Neptune.

As a teenager, I was lucky enough to experience 2 breathtaking comets in the space of a year. The first to arrive was Comet Hyakutake (*hyak-oo-tack*-eh), discovered in January 1996 by the Japanese amateur comet-hunter Yuji Hyakutake using a pair of 25 × 150 binoculars. The comet reached peak brightness in March 1996, when it was easily visible to the naked eye. I still have a grainy photograph of myself pointing towards the sky, with Comet Hyakutake and its tail shining majestically in the background.

The following year, an even more spectacular lightshow rolled into town. Comet Hale-Bopp was the brightest comet seen in many decades, dubbed the Great Comet of 1997. It truly was a magnificent sight, almost as bright as Sirius, and sporting twin tails. Its gas tail, caused by a stream of particles from the Sun—called the *solar wind*—knocking tiny bits off the comet as it passed, was long and straight. Its dust tail, caused by fragments flying off the comet, curved into a fan shape and trailed off to one side.

Fun Fact

Comet Hale-Bopp was discovered twice in July 1995. Amateur stargazer Thomas Bopp was observing with friends in a field in Arizona, USA, when he caught a glimpse of an object that wasn't on his star map. On the same night, astronomer Alan Hale was searching for comets from his driveway in New Mexico, USA, and also happened upon the fuzzy smudge in the sky. Both contacted astronomical authorities and the comet was named jointly in their honor.

What made Hale-Bopp's appearance even more amazing was that the longer tail grew to around 40 degrees in length—twice the length of Orion!

I know what you're thinking: How do I get in on the comet action? In some ways, seeing a truly great comet like Hale-Bopp comes down to luck. They show up unexpectedly every few decades, have their moment of glory in the inner solar system, and then leave, never to return—or at least not for thousands of years.

Fun Fact

Most great comets will eventually return. Hale-Bopp's orbit is estimated to take over 2500 years, and Hyakutake's more than 17,000 years. However, even if you could wait that long, there's no guarantee that they will be as bright the next time round. Comets break up and disintegrate over time, so each display is different.

Your Turn

To snag your first comet, keep an eye on astronomy news sources covering your part of the world, and regularly search your night-sky app for any comets visible where you are. Many will be faint, but any touted as binocular objects should easily be within your grasp. Happy hunting!

Fun Fact

In another impressive spacecraft cometary maneuver, in 2004 NASA flew a spacecraft named Stardust up to Comet Wild-2 and captured samples of the dust trailing off it, returning them safely to Earth for further study.

But some comets have smaller orbits and are a little more predictable. The most famous is Halley's Comet, which has shown up like clockwork every 76 years or so since it appeared in ancient Chinese records stretching back more than 2000 years. Halley's Comet will next visit Earth in the year 2062. How old will you be then?

There's no shortage of fainter comets that are visible through binoculars or a small backyard telescope. You might expect to see between 1 and 4 such comets every year. I was recently observing Comet Leonard with a small pair of binoculars from woodland near my home. I even managed to get a faint photograph of its fuzzy head and elegant curved tail with my smartphone. Not a dazzler, but an exciting target nonetheless.

Shooting stars and meteor showers

Comets are like messy eaters, leaving a string of crumbs (well, comet dust) trailing in their wake. Our planet regularly flies across these dust lanes, and when it does, a shower of tiny comet fragments hits our atmosphere. Each one burns up as a shooting star, or meteor, leaving behind a streak of light across the night sky. We call these events *meteor showers*.

Meteor showers are predictable in many ways. Firstly, we know the date of each shower. Most meteor showers last for weeks, but with a very strong peak lasting only a few hours as the Earth passes through the busiest part of the comet's orbit. At this time, the number of shooting stars is significantly higher.

We know the precise point in the sky from which the meteors will approach. This is called the *radiant*, because the meteors seem to "radiate" out in all directions. That makes meteor showers really awesome to photograph, since you can take a long-exposure photograph of many shooting stars blasting out from a central point on the sky, like a firework!

Each meteor shower is named after the constellation where the radiant sits. For example, the Orionid meteor shower peaks in October, with the radiant in Orion. The Geminids in December radiate from … you guessed it, Gemini. Look towards the radiant to see the meteors appearing to zoom out in all directions.

Look It Up

Jump online to websites like **timeanddate. com/astronomy/ meteor-shower/list. html** to find a full list of meteor showers, the phase of the moon, and whether the meteors will be bright or faint. You can also look up the dates the showers will experience their *maximum*, which is the average number of meteors you can expect to see every hour.

Your Turn

Plan ahead to view your meteor shower so you know when the next big shower is coming. If there is no meteor shower for a while, don't worry—with patience, you can always catch a sporadic meteor. These can happen at any time and come from any direction, as small pieces of space debris frequently rain down on our planet.

Fun Fact

It's rare, but when the Earth intersects an area well stocked with cometary debris, we can witness something truly spectacular: a meteor storm. On November 12 1833, a meteor storm raged over North America, with an estimated quarter of a million shooting stars appearing in the sky that night—eyewitnesses described it as "the sky raining fire." Since then, what became known as the Leonids have hit a strong peak every 3 decades or so, with storm-like conditions most recently seen in 1966, 2001, and 2002. Definitely one to watch in the coming years as we approach the next predicted peak!

Top 5 tips for observing a meteor shower

1 Do your research

Look online for the dates of upcoming meteor showers visible from where you are. A few days beforehand, go outside to make sure that the constellation where the meteor shower will appear is clearly visible, with nothing in the way. If necessary, ask a grown-up to take you to a local park for a better view.

2 Observe at the peak time

The best time to observe a meteor shower is at its peak, with the maximum number of shooting stars. Astronomy websites often list the "ZHR" (zenith hourly rate) of a meteor shower, which is the average number of shooting stars you would expect to see in an hour if the radiant were at the zenith (overhead). The best meteor showers have a maximum of around 120 meteors per hour, which is 1 every 30 seconds.

3 No telescope needed

Meteors streak across the sky very quickly, lasting a few seconds at most, so ditch those binoculars and telescopes. Simply sit, relax your eyes, and patiently look in the general direction of the radiant.

4 Avoid the Moon

The Moon is not your friend when it comes to observing a meteor shower. Some shooting stars can stand out in a moonlit sky, but many are only visible when the sky is dark. To avoid disappointment, check the phase of the Moon before heading out.

5 Take pictures

Pop your camera on a tripod, point it towards the radiant, choose a long-exposure setting, and take your photograph. The longer you leave the shutter open, the more meteors you will capture.

Fun Fact 😊

You may be lucky enough to spot a spectacularly bright meteor known as a fireball. They are quite rare but will take your breath away. Some fireballs are accompanied by colors, caused by chemicals burning up in the atmosphere. Others leave a glowing trail of light—or rarely, smoke—for a few seconds.

Asteroids

In all my years of stargazing, I've never seen an asteroid. Yet these fascinating objects have played an important role in the natural history of the Earth.

Around 66 million years ago, a smallish asteroid 6 to 9 miles wide hit the Earth and caused more than three-quarters of the planet's living species to become extinct, including most of the dinosaurs. The impact left a crater 112 miles across at the bottom of the Gulf of Mexico. Clearly, the golden rule is: Don't mess with asteroids.

Since the whole, ahem, dinosaur incident, other asteroids have come too close for comfort. On June 30, 1908, a rock the size of a soccer field entered the Earth's atmosphere near Tunguska in eastern Russia, creating a slow-moving fireball reported to be nearly as bright as the Sun. Eyewitnesses heard a noise like thunder and felt a tremendous hot wind as the rock exploded around 3 miles above the Earth's surface. A powerful shockwave flattened more than 80 million trees across about 770 square miles of forest, and shattered windows in buildings hundreds of miles away. Scientists estimate that an event like this happens every few hundred years.

So what is an asteroid? It's a large rock that lives in space. Asteroids are different from comets in several ways: They form closer to the Sun; their orbits are more circular; and their bodies contain a lot of metals, including iron, nickel, platinum, even gold.

Most asteroids live in a region between the orbits of Mars and Jupiter known as the *asteroid belt*. We have counted about a million asteroids there, but there are probably millions more that we haven't yet discovered. Occasionally, one of them is nudged from its orbit by the gravitational pull of a planet, sending it tumbling out of the asteroid belt and through the solar system. The 2 potato-shaped moons of Mars, Phobos and Deimos, are thought to be asteroids captured long ago by the gravitational field of the Red Planet.

Your Turn

Since asteroids are a lot smaller than planets and don't shine with their own light, many are pretty faint. But if you want to spot a cousin of the dinosaur-killing asteroid, at least 25 of them are visible with a pair of 10 × 50 binoculars. Start your search with Vesta, which is 330 miles wide and the brightest asteroid in the night sky. Because its surface is made of shiny volcanic rocks, it reflects a lot of sunlight and can occasionally be seen with the naked eye, if you know where to look. The best way to locate Vesta—or any asteroid—is by using the search option on your smartphone's night-sky app. Just type in the asteroid's name and the app will point you in the right direction.

Many more asteroids are visible through binoculars, including Pallas, Iris, Juno, Hygiea, and Eros. Besides having wonderful names, they are great targets for stargazers who are willing to persevere to find a small, star-like object. Now *I'm* inspired. Definitely going asteroid hunting tonight!

Fun Fact

Ceres is the largest rocky body in the asteroid belt—at around 620 miles across, it is almost twice as big as Vesta. Ceres was discovered in 1901 and for over a century it was known as an asteroid. But in 2006, it was reclassified as a minor planet, although astronomers are still arguing about exactly what the difference is. You'd better go and see for yourself!

Top 5 tips for getting to know more about comets, meteors, and asteroids

1 Start your search for comets by looking for smaller, fainter comets with a pair of binoculars.

2 Plan ahead using an online astronomical calendar to know when the best times are to view comets, meteor showers, and asteroids.

3 Take note of my top 5 tips for observing a meteor shower (see page 79).

4 Start your asteroid search by looking for the biggest and brightest asteroid, Vesta.

5 The best way to locate Vesta—or any asteroid—is by using the search option on your smartphone's night-sky app. Just type in the asteroid's name and the app will point you in the right direction.

8

SATELLITE spotting

Want to look up at night and spot a real-life spaceship? Wave at an astronaut soaring overhead? Well, if the skies are clear tonight, you just might be in luck.

For the past 4.6 billion years, our night has featured only natural objects like stars, planets, comets, asteroids, nebulae, and galaxies. Until, that is, 1957, when the Soviet Union sent the very first human-made object into space, a 23-inch metal sphere called *Sputnik*. The space age had well and truly begun.

Today, there are more than 7,000 spacecraft orbiting our planet, many of which can be seen with the naked eye as they streak across the night sky. We call them *satellites* because they are bound to Earth by gravity, just like the Moon. They range from the size of a shoebox to that of a small truck. Most satellites don't have people on board and carry equipment such as radio transmitters, cameras, and other sensors. A few are big enough to house several crew members who may live and work there for months at a time.

How to see them

How do you spot a satellite, much less figure out which ones have people on board? (Cue frantic waving!)

The best time to hunt for satellites is when the Sun has recently dipped below the horizon and the sky is starting to get dark: the time known as twilight.

You can watch them glide effortlessly in an elegant arc above your head. I often sit outside in my garden as the stars come out and watch the satellites whizz past, imagining what it's like to be up there, taking in the breathtaking view of the Earth from above.

Your Turn

Find your comfy stargazing spot (hello again, beach chair!) and settle down for a few minutes, allowing your eyes to adjust to the low light. Seek out a familiar constellation, or a planet, to get your bearings. Now relax and scan the sky for moving lights. You shouldn't have to wait for long since there are hundreds of them crossing the sky each night.

Fun Fact

Satellites are silent and have no lights on board. You can only see them because they reflect light from the Sun, so they appear steady and white. But the Sun has already set, I hear you cry! Not for the satellite, which is soaring 620 miles above the Earth's surface. It's still catching rays long after we experience sundown here at ground level.

Look It Up

All good night-sky apps contain a database of satellites. This means you can point your device at an object as it flies overhead and get an immediate identification.

Your Turn

As well as spotting satellites at random, you can plan ahead and hunt out some of the bigger, brighter, and most exciting spacecraft in the skies. Giant structures like the International Space Station, which is 358 feet long and has huge solar panels attached to it, are especially dazzling. You might be lucky enough to spot the Hubble Space Telescope if you live within 28.5 degrees of the equator, or China's Tiangong Space Station if you live between 42 degrees north and south. Don't forget to wave!

It's not just the very brightest satellites that can catch your eye. The spacecraft "constellations" (groups of satellites) are deployed in large swarms. That means you will sometimes spot a long line of bright lights, one following the next, moving across the sky. People are still getting used to this strange sight—authorities have received many calls from concerned members of the public who believe we're being invaded by aliens!

Look It Up

You can use specialist websites to plan your spacecraft viewing, including **heavens-above.com** and **N2YO.com**.

Rocket launches

If you're very lucky, you might be able to watch a rocket soar into the atmosphere on its way to launching a satellite into space. There are quite a few major launch sites around the world, including in Argentina, French Guiana, Russia, Iran, Israel, China, Canada, Japan, India, New Zealand, the United States, and Kazakhstan. Some people travel hundreds of miles to witness the spectacle of a rocket roaring into space firsthand—from a safe distance, of course. But even if you don't live close to a launch site, it's occasionally possible to see rockets blazing across the night sky as they make their way into orbit.

Swarms of spacecraft

When I started stargazing in the 1990s, it was quite rare to spot a satellite among the stars, with only 500 active satellites orbiting our planet. But in recent years their numbers have increased dramatically, with a group of rival companies launching large satellite constellations into low-Earth orbits. These satellite swarms receive internet signals from ground stations on Earth, then beam the signals back down into areas with previously poor internet connection. The plan is to eventually have tens of thousands of satellites beaming fast internet across the world. Our night sky is fast becoming a highway filled with their little trails of reflected sunlight.

Look It Up

You can also watch rocket launches online. There's oodles of information on the internet about upcoming lift-offs, try RocketLaunch.live. It's worth researching the trajectory (the path) of the rocket as it zooms across the sky, just in case it passes over your hometown. Keep your eyes peeled!

Fun Fact

Satellites are not just used for internet connections. Earth-observation spacecraft are continually monitoring our planet, with the images they take being used in weather forecasting and to predict natural disasters like volcano eruptions, floods, and tsunamis. They are also used by farmers to track crop health and manage water for irrigation, and they help us to study climate change, research the oceans, and track wildfires. This is important stuff.

Many people are asking whether we are right to spoil our precious night sky in the name of technology. It is getting harder and harder for astronomers to take pictures through a telescope and get an image that doesn't feature streaks of reflected light from satellites. This can lessen the amount of scientific information we can gather. A dark sky is also a vital part of many people's lives, especially Indigenous peoples who use the stars for navigation, sourcing food and water, and cultural events. Many regard light pollution in the night skies as an erosion of our natural environment.

Potential solutions to satellite light pollution include dabbing the satellites with anti-reflective paint, putting sun shields on them, and choosing higher orbits so that the satellites aren't as bright. But these actions will only partly reduce the amount of light that they reflect. With hundreds of thousands of satellites being planned, we need to think of new ways to reduce the impact of these spacecraft on our night sky.

Space junk

We humans have done a great job of messing up planet Earth, with plastic filling our oceans and climate change threatening our future. If that's not bad enough, we are also polluting the region above Earth's atmosphere, which has become a vast garbage dump of broken and discarded spacecraft fragments that circle our planet.

There are literally millions of pieces of junk up there, orbiting the Earth. They range in size from tiny flecks of paint to out-of-control satellites and rockets as big as a house. Orbiting Earth at speeds of up to 17,000 miles per hour, 10 times faster than a speeding bullet, even a tiny piece of this rogue debris can do enormous damage to a spacecraft. Every so often, a satellite is destroyed by a fragment of this junk, like in 2009 when 2 satellites accidentally collided, destroying both.

Scientists are now working on solutions to this messy problem, including space nets that catch the debris and lasers that nudge the pieces of junk into the Earth's atmosphere, where they would become shooting stars. The problem is, who's going to pay for it? We don't have any volunteers yet.

Your Turn

How would you fix the problem of space junk? Jot down a few ideas of your own on how to clean up space by capturing and disposing of these leftover spacecraft parts.

Top 5 facts for satellite spotting

1 The best time to hunt for satellites is when the sky is just starting to get dark: the time known as twilight.

2 All good night-sky apps contain a database of satellites. This means you can point your device at an object as it flies overhead and get an immediate identification.

3 You can use specialist websites to plan your spacecraft viewing, including heavens-above.com and N2YO.com.

4 A dark sky is a vital part of many people's lives, especially Indigenous peoples who use the stars for navigation, sourcing food and water, and cultural events.

5 We need to think of new ways to reduce the impact of spacecraft on our night sky, and scientists are working on this problem.

9
HIDDEN TREASURES
of the SKIES

Ahoy there me hearties, I have good news! Did you know that your star map is also ... a treasure map? That's right, there's a lot more to the night sky than meets the eye, and it's all there to be discovered if you know where to look. So grab a star map and together we will hunt for hidden bounty.

What are these cosmic jewels hidden in the dead of night? They are made up of millions of deep sky objects, things that are neither stars nor solar system bodies like planets, comets, moons, asteroids or minor planets. A deep sky object could be anything else in the whole universe: a cloud of space gas, a galaxy or a star cluster. Because deep sky objects are mostly faraway, faint, and fuzzy, your eyes struggle to get enough light to see interesting detail. By far the best way to observe them is with a pair of binoculars or, better still, a telescope.

Let's meet some of them now.

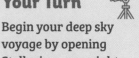

Your Turn

Begin your deep sky voyage by opening Stellarium or a night-sky app. Switch on the "deep sky objects" option and you will see a blizzard of these mysterious objects appear on the map.

Nocturnal nebulae

Let's start with a spectacular nebula that is visible wherever you are in the world.

Below Orion's belt—or, if you're in the Southern Hemisphere, above it—hangs his sword, a trio of stars. If you look very carefully at the middle star in Orion's sword, you'll notice that it isn't a star-like point of light but rather a cloudy smudge. With a pair of binoculars, you can start to see the nebulous nature of this object. This is Messier 42 (M42), commonly known as the Orion Nebula.

When I was 14 years old, I spent many hours under the night sky sketching the Orion Nebula with a pencil and paper while looking through a borrowed telescope. It was quite relaxing. I hope you will spend happy times observing it too.

Your Turn

With a decent-size telescope with a diameter of at least 150 millimeters, you should be able to make out the fine structure of the gas and see the 4 brilliant blue stars known as the Trapezium. Right now, this young star cluster is in the process of being born out of the nebula. What you can't see are the other 700 stars also beginning their lives in this gigantic star-forming nursery.

Look It Up

Look at photos of the Orion Nebula online (nasa.gov/image-feature/a-peek-inside-the-orion-nebula) and you'll see the tremendous colors given off by the gas. Look out for the wondrous Carina Nebula, which is best seen in the Southern Hemisphere, and the comically named Running Chicken Nebula in Centaurus. In northern skies, look for the North America Nebula in Cygnus—it has a bright shimmering body of glowing gas crossed by its famous dark dust band. Sadly, we can't see these colors with our eyes, because we see very faint objects in shades of gray. There are so many nebulae to explore. Search your night-sky app, get those binoculars out and start scanning the skies.

Dark, dusty corners

A very different type of space cloud is *a dark nebula.* As the name suggests, these nebulae don't shine but instead block the light from background stars. The Milky Way is full of dark nebulae, while the famous Dark Emu or Emu in the Sky that we met in Chapter 2 is a colossal chain of dark nebulae that forms an important cultural symbol for Indigenous people of the Australian continent.

In the Southern Cross, hunt for the famous Coalsack Nebula, which is also known as the head of the Dark Emu. You'll find it nestled below the bright star Acrux, or Alpha Crucis. For northern observers, the Northern Coalsack Nebula can be found close to the bright star Deneb in the constellation of Cygnus (the Swan).

Fun Fact

In the 1770s, the French comet-hunter Charles Messier (*Mess*-ee-ay) would jump up and down with excitement thinking he had discovered a comet, only to find that it was a nebula or a star cluster that had been known about for years. To avoid wasting time on wild goose chases, Messier decided to draw up his own catalogue of things that kind of look like comets but aren't. *The Messier Catalogue*, which names these objects from M1 to M110, is still used by astronomers today.

Planetary confusion

Despite how it sounds, a *planetary nebula* has nothing at all to do with planets.

Planetary nebulae are the end-stages of a star's life. When a star like our Sun runs out of fuel, it puffs up and starts shedding its outer layers of gas. The result is a big, round, glowing nebula that gradually expands into space. Planetary nebulae show off some amazing colors and occasionally form symmetrical shapes resembling a butterfly. These outlines are caused, we think, by magnetic fields shaping the gas as it expands, or by unseen companion stars swirling the gas into intricate designs. Because they are faint, planetary nebulae are invisible to the naked eye.

In Southern Hemisphere skies, the Bug Nebula (or Butterfly Nebula) lies close to the tip of Scorpius's tail. It's a wonderful sight through binoculars or a telescope, showing off its symmetrical design. Another great southern planetary nebula is the Helix Nebula in Aquarius. Through a small telescope, it looks like 2 circular puffs of smoke that are intertwined.

In Northern Hemisphere skies, the Dumbbell Nebula is the brightest object of this class. It lives in the small but cunning constellation of Vulpecula (the Fox). Through binoculars, it looks like a faint silver coin hanging in the sky. Your night-sky app will guide the way.

Another superb telescope target is M57, the Ring Nebula in the constellation of Lyra. To find it, locate the bright blue star Vega, then look for the 2 smaller stars that lie next to it: Beta and Gamma Lyrae. Directly between this pair, you'll find an almost perfectly spherical loop of ghostly light.

Fun Fact

You can see the leftovers of some of these cosmic explosions, which are called *supernova remnants*, in the night sky. Like planetary nebulae, they often appear as spherical or butterfly-shaped clouds of gas. They present challenges for binocular observers, though, since supernova remnants are notoriously faint. Even with a telescope, you will benefit from buying a nebula filter, which helps you to focus on a single color of light emitted by the oxygen atoms in the remnant. This can make them stand out more.

Supernova smoke rings

When a heavyweight star ends its life, what happens next is far more dramatic than the outer layers of gas simply puffing up and expanding into space. Stars that start out more than 8 times heavier than the Sun end their lives in a cataclysmic explosion called a *supernova*, which completely obliterates the star and leaves leftover gas rushing into space at more than 20,000 miles per second—a distance 2½ times the diameter of the Earth. Serious stuff.

With binoculars and a dark sky, you can just make out the Crab Nebula (M1) in the constellation of Taurus. Photographs taken through large telescopes show a spectacular mass of intertwined gas filaments that glow with amazing colors. This incredible object is the remnant of a colossal explosion that was first recorded by Chinese and Native American astronomers in the year 1054. Sometimes in astronomy it's not what you see, but knowing what it means that blows your mind.

If you have a telescope (especially one with the nebula filter), check out the Veil Nebula in the constellation of Cygnus. It is a vast remnant of a star that exploded more than 10,000 years ago. The leftover gases from this devastating event have now expanded into a region 6 times wider than the full Moon. There are no written records of the supernova explosion itself, but scientists calculate that, at the time, it would have appeared brighter than Venus. Spectacular indeed!

Fun Fact

When hunting for faint objects in the night sky, look slightly away from center. You might be surprised at how much brighter your target looks. The retina of your eye has 2 types of light receptors: rods and cones. Rods are great at detecting faint light but don't see color. Cones give us color vision but they're bad at picking up faint light. The middle of your retina is packed with cones, which means your night vision is less sensitive when you look directly at something.

Stupendous star clusters

Stars don't just magically appear in space. They are born when gigantic clouds of gas squish together (that's a scientific term) under the force of gravity. This causes pockets of hot gas to form, which eventually turn into stars and planets. When the gas clears and the newborn stars begin to shine through, these regions become *open clusters*.

We met the most spectacular open cluster in the night sky—the Pleiades—in Chapter 3. But there are many more of these beautiful objects to share. Let's meet some now:

In northern skies, the constellation of Cancer (the Crab) hosts the Beehive Cluster. To the naked eye it looks cloudy—and its true nature is unclear. But viewed through binoculars, it crystallizes as a cluster of brilliant bluey-white stars.

Heading south, the Jewel Box Cluster in the Southern Cross is a worthy destination, if not for the number of stars then for their bedazzling colors. Similarly, both NGC 3532 and the Southern Pleiades, both in the constellation of Carina (the Keel), provide a mesmerizing display to explore through a small telescope.

Close to the stinging tail of Scorpius lies the Ptolemy Cluster (M7). A naked-eye object, this large, open cluster (2 full Moons wide) is a stellar nursery filled with intensely blue stars. Just 5 degrees (3 fingers) from the Ptolemy Cluster lies M6, the Butterfly Cluster. They are so close together that you should be able to fit both into a binocular's field of view. The Butterfly Cluster is somewhat smaller than Ptolemy, but still visible to the unaided eye. Among a large selection of standard bluey-white stars in this cluster is the odd one out—the giant orange star BM Scorpii (sc*orp-ee-i*). See if you can spot it.

Another type of star cluster is made up of very old stars. We call them *globular clusters* because the stars are squashed together into a tight ball that looks like a globe. Amazingly, these are often made up of many hundreds of thousands, if not millions, of stars. The individual stars in these clusters can be older than 13 billion years. Imagine having to buy candles for *that* birthday cake!

6 out of the 7 brightest globular clusters are in the southern skies. The most spectacular candidates are Omega Centauri (in Centaurus) and 47 Tucanae (too-*carn*-ee) in Tucana (the Toucan), both of which are faintly visible to the naked eye. Omega Centauri is the brightest globular cluster in the whole sky, containing around 10 million stars. How do we know? We count the light, not the individual stars. Phew!

Your Turn

Use your favorite night-sky app to find Omega Centauri. A pair of binoculars—or better still, a small telescope—will reveal a tightly packed nest of stars that covers an area almost as large as the full Moon. Some liken it to a swarm of bees. Almost as impressive is 47 Tucanae, which covers a similar area and is almost as bright. If you like a challenge, give M22 in Sagittarius a whirl. Although slightly smaller and fainter than the clusters I mentioned before, it still makes a tremendous sight.

Globular clusters in the northern sky can't compete with the likes of Omega Centauri, but they do offer some pretty good binocular targets. Try any from this list: M5 in Serpens, M13 in Hercules, M3 in Canes Venatici and M15 in Pegasus. All can be seen from urban areas with a decent pair of binoculars, although they are quite a bit fainter and less than half the apparent size of the great southern globular clusters of Omega Centauri and 47 Tucanae. Fair enough too—they are a lot further away.

The Milky Way

You may notice a thick band, or something that looks like a river, of stars streaming across the night sky. We call this the *Milky Way*. It is most spectacular when viewed under a very dark sky, but you can still make it out from darker places in towns and cities like parks, beaches, or wooded areas. The Milky Way is our own galaxy, home to around 200 billion stars, including the Sun. It is flat like a pancake, and that's why we see it from the inside as a faint cosmic highway streaking across the night sky.

Glittering galaxies

There are trillions of other galaxies in the universe, but only the closest few are visible to the naked eye. In the southern sky or from the tropics, you might notice 2 faintly glowing patches of white light shimmering above your head. You'd be forgiven for mistaking them for clouds, but they are in fact 2 small galaxies made up of billions of stars. We call them the *Small Magellanic Cloud* and the *Large Magellanic Cloud*.

Another member of our cosmic clan is the nearby spiral galaxy M31, the Andromeda Galaxy, which is visible from almost anywhere in the world. It's amazing to think that we can spot it with the naked eye when it is around 2 million light-years (12 million trillion miles) away! That's how bright the combined light of a trillion stars can be. The spiral shape of Andromeda closely matches that of our own galaxy, but since we see it partially edge-on, it appears slightly squashed, like a football that has been sat on by a cute but clumsy labrador.

Another large spiral galaxy in the local group is M33, the Triangulum Galaxy. You can spot it with the naked eye if you're lucky enough to enjoy dark skies. If not, binoculars should reveal its faint shimmer.

Back in Southern Hemisphere or tropical skies, the peculiar galaxy Centaurus A is a worthy target. It is best viewed through a telescope of at least 200 millimeters in diameter, which reveals a dark band of dust visible against the bright halo of light shining from millions of stars. Some call it the Hamburger Galaxy, with the dusty band representing the burger and the bright halo of stars the bun!

Galaxies are a fascinating target for backyard astronomers, especially those with telescopes. But anyone can get started with the naked-eye Magellanic clouds in the southern sky or the Andromeda Galaxy in the north. So rev your engines and get started on your intergalactic journey.

Top 5 tips on discovering the hidden treasures of the skies

1 With the naked eye you can see the Milky Way, our home galaxy, as a band of stars across the night sky.

2 A nebula is a cloud of gas in space—some are dark and others glow in magnificent colors.

3 With binoculars you can explore many bright star clusters, most of which are made up of hot, young blue or white stars.

4 Some stars end their lives in an explosion called a supernova, leaving leftover gas rushing into space, which you can spot through a telescope.

5 In globular clusters, hundreds of thousands of old, red stars are squashed together into a tight ball, which you can see with binoculars.

10

The SUN

Everyone loves the Sun. Without it, the Earth would be a cold, dark, frozen rock floating gloomily through space. Sure, maybe that would be good for stargazing, with no light pollution, but it would be extremely bad for human beings. No sunlight equals no plants, no animals, and no us. I'd rather our planet didn't become a popsicle, thank you very much.

The Sun might be a nuisance to astronomers, blotting out the stars during the daytime, but it's interesting in its own right. There are many features to explore, and the Sun's interactions with planets, moons, and our atmosphere can create beautiful results. With a bit of practice, you can learn how to spot some of our star's greatest party tricks!

Sunspots

The Sun is made of a weird, extremely hot, gas-like substance called plasma. Heat rises from the middle of the Sun, bringing with it great globs of this stuff. The plasma rises up to the surface of the Sun (called the *photosphere*) before sinking back into the depths.

This whole process is kept in line by magnetic forces generated deep inside the Sun, which can push hot plasma beneath the surface, causing a cooler, darker patch on the Sun called a *sunspot*. I say "cooler"—it's at 6,700 degrees Fahrenheit, as opposed to 9,900 degrees across the rest of the Sun's surface. Don't touch the sunspots.

The Sun goes through a *solar cycle* approximately every eleven years, which is linked to changes in the magnetic activity of the Sun. During it, we see lots of sunspots for a couple of years, then the numbers gradually drop until we see hardly any, then the cycle repeats. The current solar cycle is expected to peak between 2024 and 2026, and the number of sunspots has so far exceeded expectations, so it's a great time to be searching for solar activity.

Looking directly at the Sun for even a second can cause catastrophic damage to your eyesight, so never do it. The only completely safe way to observe the Sun is by projecting its image onto a light colored surface, like a piece of paper.

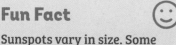

Look It Up

Look online to find videos of our star bubbling like a hot pan of soup.

Fun Fact

Sunspots vary in size. Some are a few miles across, and the largest can grow to more than 62,000 miles across, which is many times bigger than the Earth. They shrink and grow depending on the magnetic conditions on the Sun, but most fade after a few days or weeks.

As a teenager, I saw my very first sunspots using binoculars with this safe method. Here's how you can do it too:

1 Cut a piece of cardboard to size and place it around the middle of the binoculars like a skirt to create a sun shade.

2 Without looking through them, attach the binoculars to a tripod and point them in the general direction of the Sun —keeping your back to the Sun.

3 Roughly 12–20 inches from the eyepiece, hold a piece of white paper attached to a clipboard—or any flat surface will do. Slowly move the binoculars around until they line up with the Sun.

4 When you've hit the right spot, the bright image of the Sun will appear on the piece of paper.

5 Move the paper closer to or farther away from the eyepiece, to bring the Sun's image into sharp focus. When focused, it will look like a big yellow circle on the sheet of paper. Looking closer at the image, hunt for any small black dots on the paper.

> **Fun Fact**
>
> At *solar minimum*, there are sometimes no sunspots at all, whereas at *solar maximum*, the daily number of sunspots can range from 50 up to as many as 200. A Sun that spotty is an incredible sight.

Ta da! Sunspots.

It's incredible to think that a small black speck on the Sun's disk is actually a gigantic well on the surface of our nearest star that is as big as planet Earth.

You can project an image of the Sun in the same way using a telescope. Or you can use a piece of cardboard with a pinhole punched in the middle. The tiny hole projects an image of the

Sun onto a piece of white paper, without using a lens. It's called a pinhole camera, about which you can find tutorials online. Just remember to never, under any circumstances, look directly at the Sun.

Look It Up

Want to check out the Sun's activity? Visit NASA's Solar Dynamics Observatory website **sdo.gsfc.nasa.gov/data** for real-time views from a spacecraft orbiting the Earth. Sunspots are best seen on the yellow-and-orange filtered images.

Your Turn

You can do your own scientific experiment using the motion of sunspots to measure the rotation of the Sun. Mark the positions of sunspots on a piece of paper a few hours apart, and use this observation to figure out how long it takes for the Sun to spin around once on its axis. Try it for yourself!

Aurorae

The magnetic activity of the Sun creates more than just sunspots. It also produces exciting outbursts like *solar flares*, which are hot plasma eruptions where the Sun sends a large burp of gas into space. Oooo … pardon me.

This gas pours down towards Earth at the North and South Magnetic Poles—these are close to, but not right at, the geographical poles. The Sun's burped gas collides with gases in our atmosphere, lighting up the sky in flickering, cascading displays of vivid reds, greens, and purples. We call this lightshow an *aurora* (or-*roar*-ra). For more than one aurora, we use the word *aurorae* (or-*roar*-ree).

The aurora borealis (northern lights) are visible from Canada, Alaska, and northern parts of Europe and Russia. The aurora australis (southern

Your Turn

If an aurora is forecast, find a clear, dark spot and point your camera towards the north horizon if you live in the Northern Hemisphere, or the south horizon, if you live in the Southern Hemisphere. My favorite location in Australia is a south-facing beach with no artificial lights on the water. Take a test shot with an exposure time of 20–30 seconds, which should pick up any faint auroral colors that your eyes can't see. If you're lucky enough to spot an aurora on your photograph, keep snapping away, because the aurora's light show can change from minute to minute. One of my most treasured astronomy keepsakes is a time-lapse video of a spectacular aurora in 2020, which captured the display's ever-changing features.

Fun Fact

Did you know that other planets have aurorae? When the Sun spits out a large solar flare, the entire solar system can be affected. The giant planets Jupiter, Saturn, Uranus, and Neptune are all known to experience auroral displays. Imagine how incredible it would be to sit on one of Saturn's moons and look across to the ringed planet, taking in the sight of its shimmering curtains of auroral light.

lights) are generally confined to southern parts of Australia, New Zealand, and South America.

Although we can see (with spacecraft) when a glob of solar plasma is on its way, the aurora is still quite unpredictable, so you can't always tell exactly where and when it will appear. If you live in the aurora zone, keep an eye on the online "space weather" forecasts for your location.

Solar eclipses

We have already learned about lunar eclipses, in which, over the course of a few hours, the Earth's shadow creeps across the full Moon's face and then retreats again. Solar eclipses are something quite different. A total solar eclipse happens at the new Moon, when the Moon appears to completely cover the Sun. It's a celestial peekaboo of epic proportions, plunging a small part of the Earth's surface into darkness in the middle of the day.

>
> **Fun Fact**
>
> The distance between the Earth and the Moon varies throughout any month. If a solar eclipse happens when the Moon is farthest from the Earth, it appears slightly too small to cover the whole of the Sun and a thin ring of sunlight is visible around the Moon's edge. We call this an *annular eclipse*, also known as a "ring of fire."

It's truly amazing that the Moon and Sun fit so snugly together for this game of cosmic hide-and-seek. By a complete coincidence, the Sun is 400 times bigger but also 400 times farther away than the Moon. At the fullest part of the eclipse (called *totality*), the Moon almost perfectly covers the disk of the Sun.

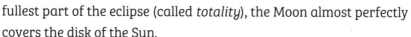

Why is this good? Well, just above the Sun is a region of swirling, tumbling gases that spew from its active surface. It's called the *chromosphere*, and this area boasts exciting features like *prominences* and solar flares. Beyond this layer is the Sun's *corona*, a thin but intensely hot glowing atmosphere whose temperature is estimated at 1.8 million degrees Fahrenheit. Normally we can't see the Sun's chromosphere or corona, because our star's dazzling surface hides these quiet whispers of light. But during a total solar eclipse, its secrets are finally uncovered.

When I was a college student, I traveled with some friends to the south-western tip of England to witness a total solar eclipse.

On the morning of August 11, 1999, the new Moon passed slowly across the face of the Sun, plunging our campsite into an eerie darkness. The warm summer's day cooled noticeably, and birds tweeted furiously as if it were bedtime. My friends and I held hands and danced in a circle. Then the Sun returned.

Look It Up

For a full list of upcoming eclipses, visit the website timeanddate.com/eclipse.

Total solar eclipses like this are extremely rare, because the size of the Moon's shadow as it tracks across the Earth is very small. Partial and annular eclipses happen more frequently. These are brilliant targets too—you can project the image of the Sun onto a piece of paper and watch its shape change as the Moon passes across its front.

Planetary transits

Mercury and Venus sometimes attempt a little solar eclipse of their own. The only trouble is that these planets are respectively around 22 times and 109 times farther away than the Moon when they do it. Instead of artfully disguising the Sun's disk and revealing the glorious glow of the corona, they merely adorn the Sun with a small, round pimple. In a matter of a few hours, the show is over.

Transits of Mercury happen every decade or so. The next time you'll be able to see our solar system's littlest rocky planet darting across the Sun's face is on November 13, 2032, then on November 7, 2039. It's a long time between shows, so don't miss it.

If you're hoping to spot a transit of Venus, you'll have to wait a little while longer. The last one was in 2012. On that day, I visited a school in Western Sydney, Australia, to talk to the students about what was happening. We projected an image of the Sun onto a giant sheet of white paper and watched as Venus's perfect little disk crept across it. The next time Venus transits the Sun will be on December 11, 2117, when I'll be just shy of my 138th birthday—it's just as well as I saw the transit in 2012!

Where do you think you will be when the next transit of Venus happens?

Top 5 things to know about the Sun

1 Fascinating features of the Sun include sunspots, prominences, and solar flares.

2 Looking directly at the Sun for even a second can cause catastrophic damage to your eyesight, so never do it. You can observe the Sun safely by projecting its image onto a piece of paper.

3 Total solar eclipses happen when the Moon passes in front of the Sun. They are rare, because the size of the Moon's shadow as it tracks across the Earth is very small.

4 NASA's Solar Dynamics Observatory website (**sdo.gsfc.nasa. gov/data**) is a great place to visit for real-time views of the Sun.

5 Sometimes, Mercury or Venus pass in front of the Sun— called a transit. The next transit of Mercury is in 2032, but Venus won't transit again until 2117.

11

STARGAZING for LIFE

On our journey together through this book, we have learned how to experience the many wonders of the night sky. We've met sparkling stars, picturesque planets, and magnificent moons. We've navigated by the constellations and dreamed of long-awaited eclipses, meteor showers, and planetary transits. Comets and aurorae have surprised us. Asteroids have alarmed us. It's all in a day's work for an astronomer.

For some, astronomy will become a lifelong hobby to share with friends and family. For others, it might even lead to a career. As a 12-year-old, I got hooked on exploring the night sky and ended up becoming a professional astrophysicist, studying the universe as my job. It has been a great source of joy throughout my life and has led me to places I never expected.

Cosmic pathways

Astronomy can take you in so many directions. You can become a scientist who uses the world's biggest telescopes to answer deep questions about the nature of stars, galaxies, and black holes. You can build space telescopes, Mars rovers, or planetary probes to study the history of our solar system. You can use mathematics to test the most out-there possibilities of how the universe works. You can build rockets and satellites or even travel in space! Best of all, you get to work with people from all over the world to solve exciting puzzles. What could be better?

To get into professional astronomy, you will need to study mathematics and physics so that you can understand how to unravel the mysteries of the cosmos. You should learn how to write computer code, and how to work well with others. You will need to learn to write clearly and give presentations as well as listen, so that you can share your results and learn what other people have found in their research.

Engineers also work in astronomy. They create tools and machines that help us to measure the universe. Engineers build great telescopes on mountaintops, in remote deserts, even at the South Pole! Software engineers and data scientists code computers to make sense of the information that these telescopes gather, and they turn invisible signals from outer space, like X-rays and radio waves, into pictures that we can see and understand.

You are a scientist

Backyard astronomers make hugely important discoveries every day. Many comets are unearthed by regular people using small telescopes or binoculars. These discoveries are deservedly named after them. Supernovae are spotted by dedicated stargazers photographing distant galaxies. Everyone has the opportunity to make groundbreaking discoveries. Who knows where your hobby could take you?

Look It Up

Jump online at **zooniverse.org** to browse a whole host of scientific challenges that you can help with.

Fun Fact

A few years ago, I was a presenter on the Australian television series *Stargazing Live*. My colleagues created a website where our viewers could hunt for undiscovered planets around nearby stars using measurements from the Kepler space telescope. Within days, 26-year-old Andrew Gray, a motor mechanic from Darwin, had discovered a new solar system with at least 5 planets. You can hunt for planets, black holes, galaxies, and mysterious bursts from space using information gathered by professional telescopes.

Friends in high places

Astronomy is a very popular hobby. There are thousands of astronomy clubs and societies all over the world. I joined my local astronomy group when I was around 13 after my dad saw an advert in a library. Mom took me to the next meeting, and everyone was so friendly and willing to share their knowledge and their telescopes.

Look It Up

Check online to see if you can find an astronomy club or society near you. If so, join in! If not, consider joining an online community to find others who share your passion for the astronomical world.

The group invited experts to talk about their favorite topics. We visited science museums and the London Planetarium. We had observing nights at a local observatory. One member lent me his 250-millimeter Dobsonian telescope for a month, allowing me to explore planets and deep sky objects I had never seen before. I highly recommend joining your local astronomy society to build up your own skills and knowledge about the night sky.

When I was 15 years old, I joined a program called Space School UK, a summer camp for kids interested in astronomy—many other countries have something similar. We stayed on a university campus in London for 5 days and took part in a program of fascinating talks, activities, and projects. We even visited a factory that was building a satellite destined to be launched into space! It was an incredible experience, and I made friends for life, many of whom are now professional astronomers like me.

Here for the beauty

Anyone can fall in love with astronomy, just as I did all those years ago. It can happen after a few dark nights under a canopy of stars, a glimmer of the thin crescent Moon in the evening, or with a cheery wave to the astronauts on the International Space Station. Stargazing touches us all, through the magnificent astronomical events that we witness and the enduring memories of what the Moon, the planets, and the stars have meant to generations of our ancestors.

Seek adventure

Want my advice? Embrace our cosmic neighborhood as part of your daily life. Seek adventure in the near-infinite void beyond our Earth's atmosphere. Take the time to explore astronomy in the real world. Make friends with the stars, planets, and constellations

that tell the stories of our ancestors. Break out of the warm, cozy cocoon of your home and step out under the glorious dome of stars. Breathe it in. Enjoy how it feels to walk among 100 billion galaxies and experience more of our cosmos than most people ever will. Marvel in its many wonders. Connect with it. And good luck with your adventures.

NOTES for the INTERESTED READER

The Greek alphabet

In astronomy, the Greek alphabet is used to name the stars in a constellation from brightest to faintest, until we run out of Greek letters. For example, Alpha Orionis is the brightest star in Orion, and Gamma Crucis is the third-brightest star in Crux. It's easy when you know how! See the list below.

Some stars also have their own names, like Polaris, Betelgeuse, and Rigel. These come from a mix of the old Roman, Greek, and Arabic names for stars.

α alpha	ν nu
β beta	ξ xi
γ gamma	o omicron
δ delta	π pi
ε epsilon	ρ rho
ζ zeta	σ sigma
η eta	τ tau
θ theta	υ upsilon
ι iota	φ phi
κ kappa	χ chi
λ lambda	ψ psi
μ mu	ω omega

Fun fact: the word "alphabet" comes from the first 2 letters of the Greek alphabet, alpha and beta!

The magnitude system

Around 2,000 years ago, astronomers first came up with a system to describe the brightness of stars, planets, and deep sky objects. They called it the magnitude system, and the name stuck.

The magnitude system is odd for a couple of reasons. First, the numbers run backwards, so the larger the magnitude, the fainter the star. Weird.

The second thing that takes a bit of getting used to is that the system doesn't progress as a normal sequence of numbers, where 2 is twice as big as 1. Nope. Instead, each magnitude is 2.512 times more/less than the previous one. For example, a magnitude 3 star is 2.512 times brighter than a magnitude 4 star, and a magnitude 0 star is 2.512 times brighter than a magnitude 1 star. Get it?

Despite these oddities, the system works well and is used widely around the world by professional and amateur astronomers alike. You are likely to regularly encounter magnitudes as you read more about astronomy.

Depending on how light-polluted your sky is, the faintest object visible to the naked eye has a magnitude of roughly +6. The brightest star in the sky (Sirius) has a magnitude of –1.5. Venus can reach a magnitude of –4.6 and the full Moon has a magnitude of –12.6.

Don't be fooled, though. There are 2 types of magnitude. Here, we are talking about *apparent magnitude* (m), or how bright something appears from here on the Earth. The other type is *absolute magnitude* (M), or how bright something looks from a distance of 10 parsecs, or 186 trillion miles. This is less useful to amateur astronomers, but it's helpful to understand how bright the object really is shining.

The meridian: it's a high point

Have you ever noticed that the Sun shines brightest around the middle of the day?

Every day, the planets and stars (including the Sun) move across the sky as the Earth rotates. They reach their highest point in the sky as they cross the *meridian*, an imaginary line that starts from due north on the horizon, rises directly overhead, and arcs back down to due south. Have a go at tracing the meridian right now: Find north and south on your horizon and trace an arc with your finger up above your head, joining the 2.

To explore the meridian, plant a stick in the ground (or use a tree trunk if you have a lot of space) and mark the direction and length of its shadow every hour or so. As the Sun rises in the east, it will cast a long shadow towards the west. As the Sun gets higher in the sky, it moves towards the north if you're in the Southern Hemisphere or south if you're in the Northern Hemisphere. The shadow it casts gets shorter and swings around again towards the meridian. As evening comes, the Sun is once again low in the sky, this time in the west, and your trusty stick will cast a looooong shadow in an easterly direction.

It was by doing exactly these kinds of experiments that our scientist ancestors figured out that the Earth spins on its axis and moves around the Sun. Maybe you'll follow in their footsteps.

The great sky bottom

Did you know that the sky has a top and a bottom? Technically, they're called the *zenith* and the *nadir*, respectively. The zenith is the imaginary point in the sky that lies directly above your head, and the nadir is the imaginary point directly below your feet. You can't see the stars down there, of course—unless you dig a very deep hole and peer through the Earth—but you can open your night-sky app or online star map to explore them virtually, even during the daytime. What fun!

Orbital jargon

No celestial body has a perfectly circular orbit. They have elliptical (egg-shaped) orbits, meaning there is always a point where the 2 bodies are at their closest approach and a point where they are furthest apart.

For the Moon as it orbits the Earth, the closest point is called the *perigee* and the farthest is the *apogee*. In ancient Greek, *peri* means "near" and *apo* means "away from." The final part of the word (*gee*) is linked to "geo," meaning "of the Earth." Other "geo" words are geography and geothermal.

For the planets orbiting the Sun, the closest point to our star is called the *perihelion* and the farthest point is the *aphelion*. The *helion* part of these words is derived from the ancient Greek word Helios, meaning "the Sun."

Finally, for the orbits of 2 or more stars, we use the word *periastron* to describe the closest point and *apastron* for the farthest approach in the orbit. Here, *astron* means "a star," or celestial body, in ancient Greek.

RESOURCES

Websites

For an interactive view of the sky at any time and from any location on the Earth:
stellarium-web.org

Listen to what pictures from NASA's telescopes sound like:
chandra.si.edu/sound

Pick a perfect stargazing location near you with this dark-places map:
darksitefinder.com

Find out when certain planets will be visible where you live:
earthsky.org

See detailed drawings of the Moon's phases:
moon.nasa.gov

Check when the Moon rises and sets where you live:
timeanddate.com/moon

Explore the Moon's mountains, craters, and plains in all their glory:
google.com/moon
lunar.gsfc.nasa.gov

To help plan your next spacecraft viewing:
heavens-above.com
N2YO.com

Find information on upcoming rocket launches:
RocketLaunch.live

See what the Sun looks like from a spacecraft orbiting Earth:
sdo.gsfc.nasa.gov/data

To find a full list of upcoming eclipses:
timeanddate.com/eclipse

Thanks to our newest telescope, we have more pretty pictures of the cosmos:
jwst.nasa.gov/

Check the International Meteor Organization's calendar for your next meteor shower:
imo.net/resources/calendar/

An audio-described planetarium show:
audiouniverse.org/

Find out the current lunar phase:
timeanddate.com/moon/phases

Look up the position of planets in your area tonight:
timeanddate.com/astronomy/night

Explore the surface of the Moon:
quickmap.lroc.asu.edu

Find out when the International Space Station will be flying over
your location next:
spotthestation.nasa.gov

Look up the location of the Starlink satellites, a mega-constellation
of spacecraft that beam fast wi-fi to Earth:
findstarlink.com

A great source of international astronomy and space news,
including articles on how to get started with stargazing:
space.com

Night-sky apps

Sky Guide
SkyView
Stellarium
Star Walk
Night Sky
Star Chart
SkyWiki
Sky Map
NightCap Camera
ProShot

GLOSSARY

Asteroid belt
A region between the orbits of Mars and Jupiter where lots of asteroids live.

Astronomy
The study and science of things past Earth's atmosphere, such as planets, galaxies, and stars.

Astrophotography
Taking photographs of the stars.

Aurora (plural is aurorae)
A light show in the sky created by particles from the Sun colliding with Earth's atmosphere.

Atmosphere
The gases that surround a planet, moon, or other large astronomical body.

Atom
A microscopic collection of particles that is the building block of most things, including you and me!

Axis
An invisible line that an object, such as Earth, rotates or spins around.

Black hole
An object in space whose pull of gravity is so strong that light can't escape.

Celestial body
A natural object found in space, such as a meteor, planet, star, or comet. Celestial means "of the sky" in Latin.

Constellation
A group of stars that appear like a pattern. They are often named and if you drew imaginary lines to connect the stars they can look like animals, people, or objects.

Deep sky objects
Faint and hard-to-see distant objects like galaxies, gas clouds, and star clusters.

Eclipses
There are 2 types of eclipses. A lunar eclipse is when the Earth is lined up directly between the Sun and the Moon and the Moon disappears into the Earth's shadow. A solar eclipse is when the Sun disappears behind the Moon.

Equator
An imaginary circle around the middle of Earth that divides it into 2 hemispheres—the Northern Hemisphere and the Southern Hemisphere.

Ices
Frozen materials left over from the formation of the solar system. They are often found in comets, or on planets and moons.

Light pollution

When the night sky is brightened by human-made lights and you can't see as many stars. It is bad for animals as it can affect their natural cycle of day and night, which they use to feed, navigate, breed, migrate, and sleep.

Light-year

The distance that light travels in 1 year, which is equal to 9.46 trillion kilometres or 5.88 trillion miles.

Magnetic field

A region surrounding a magnetic object, where other magnetized materials are pulled or pushed by an invisible force.

Meridian

An imaginary line between the North and South Poles.

Meteor showers

When the Earth passes through a swarm of space dust and many shooting stars leave behind streaks of light in the night sky.

Milky Way

The galaxy that our solar system is in, including Earth and us.

Magnitude

What astronomers use to measure the brightness of an object in the sky, such as stars and planets.

Naked eye

Not using any equipment (like binoculars or telescopes) to look at the night sky: it's just your eyes.

Nebula (plural is nebulae)
A gigantic cloud of gases and dust particles in space.

Opposition
When a planet is directly opposite the Sun as seen from the Earth. It is similar to a full Moon and is generally the best time to look for the planet in the night sky.

Orbit
The path an object takes when it goes around another object because of gravity, such as the Earth going around the Sun or a spacecraft going around the Earth.

Plasma
Very similar to gas but so hot that the atoms are broken up into smaller particles. The Sun and stars are made of plasma.

Radiant
The imaginary point in the sky where the shooting stars come from during a meteor shower.

Sunspot
A darker patch on the surface of the Sun. It seems darker than the rest of the Sun because it is cooler, although it's still nearly 6,700 degrees Fahrenheit!

Supernova (plural is supernovae)
A massive explosion that can happen when a very big star is at the end of its life.

Zenith
The imaginary point in the sky that lies directly above your head.

INDEX

ACKNOWLEDGEMENTS

The author is grateful to the talented team who brought this book to life, particularly Sally Heath, Phil Campbell, Lisa Schuurman, Paul Smitz, Kristin Gill, and the fabulous Sophie Beer. Thanks to everyone at Thames & Hudson Australia and beyond who worked to turn a plain electronic manuscript into a beautifully illustrated book that can be enjoyed by young people around the world.

Finally, my heartfelt thanks go to you, my dear reader, for enjoying the night sky with me and protecting it for future generations.

About the author

Lisa Harvey-Smith is an award-winning astrophysicist and a professor at the University of New South Wales. With research interests in the birth and death of stars and supermassive black holes, Lisa also serves on the Australian Space Agency's Advisory Group. She previously worked on developing the Square Kilometre Array—a continent-spanning next-generation radio telescope that will survey billions of years of cosmic history.

Lisa has a talent for making complicated science seem simple and fun and is a presenter on the popular television show Stargazing Live, a guest on BBC's *The Sky at Night* and *The Infinite Monkey Cage*, and a regular science commentator on TV and radio.

Lisa has written 5 popular science books: *The Secret Life of Stars, When Galaxies Collide, Aliens and Other Worlds, Little*

Book, BIG Universe, and the bestselling children's book *Under the Stars: Astrophysics for Bedtime.* She has performed extensively in theaters with her self-penned *When Galaxies Collide* show and has appeared alongside Apollo-missions astronauts including Buzz Aldrin.

As Australia's Women in STEM Ambassador, Lisa is responsible for increasing the participation of women and girls in Science, Technology, Engineering, and Mathematics (STEM) studies and careers across Australia. She is also a vocal advocate for building inclusive workplaces for LGBTQI+ scientists. In her spare time, Lisa runs ultra-marathons, including multi-day, 12-hour and 24-hour races. She once ran 155 miles across Australia's Simpson Desert.

To find out more, visit **lisaharveysmith.com**

More books by Lisa Harvey-Smith:

About the illustrator

Sophie Beer is an author and illustrator who revels in color, shape, and texture. Living by one simple rule—art should never be boring—she primarily works in children's and editorial illustrations. Her clients include Google, Disney/Pixar, *The Guardian*, *The Boston Globe*, Hardie Grant Egmont, Scholastic UK, Penguin Random House Australia, Simon & Schuster New York, and many more. When she's not illustrating and writing, she thinks a lot about books, animals, and equality.